A Crystal Ball
VISIONING

Unfolding the 21st Century

Imad F. Abdullah, AIA

A Crystal Ball Visioning: Unfolding the 21st Century

Published by Wheatmark®
1760 East River Road, Suite 145
Tucson, Arizona 85718 USA
www.wheatmark.com

ISBN: 978-1-60494-696-3
LCCN: 2012934499

Contents

Introduction

"THE CRYSTAL BALL GREETINGS and Annual Review" was first written in December 1999 in contemplation of the year 2000 hype that became known as Y2K, with the potential self-destruction of all computers that were based on the old 8 digits system once the calendar flipped to the new century at midnight on December 31, 2000. It evolved into an annual year-end review and greetings to friends and colleagues interpreting and interpolating the events of the time and what's between the lines, and reflecting on the unforeseen future.

Since most readers will remember more vividly the recent years, the book starts with the year 2011 and goes back in time thereafter year after year through 1999. The chapters can be read independently and some may like to start with the last chapter and move forward to 2011.

Though the English language is quite structured and defined on grammar and standards of writing, the author took the liberty to maximize the poetic effect of the language and the imagery that it affords, and used some capital letters and quotations marks to highlight specific ideas and relationships within sentences. The approach is to help the reader capture the vision behind the words to reach the deep implied meanings and the predictions and thoughts as the text flows from one concept to another.

As an Architect in private practice for over 35 years and a world traveler, the author brings a truly diverse perspective on our times and interprets events and life concepts with style and ingenuity. This book is dedicated to all who live the experience of their times everywhere and who capture the moments of significance of our world and look for the intelligent interpretations and contributions of capable minds.

Imad F. Abdullah, Architect AIA
Houston, Texas

The Year 2011

2011: WHAT A YEAR IT has been, and what a global village we live in. So near yet so far, so fascinating yet so tangled up with nuclear power plants meltdowns, natural disasters, super floods, revolutions, regime changes, and countries split apart.

Japan had to deal with the ultimate nightmare as the world watched in horror the blow-out of a nuclear reactor building. Incredible as it may seem, the brave Japanese went inside to take care of business, facing their unknown fate and whether they will become irradiating radioactive elements themselves. The masses were evacuated far away from the deadly glow haunted by the shadows of the nuclear of two generations ago.

It has been almost a year now and it is getting under control, but the outcry by advocates of alternative energies continues over the whole concept of nuclear energy and the transportation of its waste and how it is eternally stored, and whether it is headed long term out of control.

Predicting natural forces that cause such events

and when and how has been elusive, but scientists think it may be possible to forecast the volcanoes and tsunamis, especially around the Ring of Fire at the perimeter of the Pacific Ocean circling the Americas and Asia. All around the ring of fire, they suggest that a change in the curvature of the earth crust occurs when both magnetic forces and solar activity intensify on the northern side of our galaxy. When both converge, the curve changes and the joints dislocate, the hot lava blows out as ferocious volcanoes and the shift of the massive tectonic plates causes earthquakes, the undersea engine for ravaging tsunamis.

Moving to politics, world events were in a race all year and we're barely catching our breath towards the end of the year as few have found their way to the end of the race. US fighting forces just left Iraq after 9 years, and the military hardware is still looking to park itself close enough to the next crisis. Getting it to Afghanistan is a costly proposition but may be a wise choice. In Iraq the coalition government is still in place yet so fragile, as the country picks up the development pace and remains on edge with dissenting leading strongmen and periodic explosions by suicidal madmen.

Looking at Afghanistan, one can follow on the maps a connecting continuous corridor starting at the northeast corner of Afghanistan where it joins China and running practically straight through Pakistan, Iran, Iraq and then Syria to reach the Mediterranean. Breaking the line with military presence in Afghanistan was deemed a strategic option for the US as it tries to secure energy from the nearby largest world sources for the black gold, a costly stretch for the US to the opposite end of the globe.

Though temperature in the Arab World is hot most of the time, the Arab Spring tempered rulers and toppled governments. Revolutions are known by this acronym since they turn everything upside down and create a revolving door for revolutionaries and various factions to go through from side to side, and once blood is in the streets it creates a one-way street. For Libya's Qaddafi the street was a dead end, where at its end he met death and his dynasty's end. Unfortunately it cost 50,000 lives and widespread destruction, a very high price to pay to stir world conscience into mobilizing support with external intervention.

Libya's revolution proved very expensive in human cost and overall destruction, and the country is trying to reign in chaos and collect arms from the rebels, and to account for what may have disappeared or sold on the black market. Qaddafi's arsenal was stout and advanced, dream type weapons for outlaws worldwide. Add to the mix the strong showing of fundamentalism, and it will be some time before stabilization re-stitches the tribal divide.

It all started from Tunisia, where a human torch lit up the skies and ushered in the Arab Spring: in desperation and anger, a Tunisian burned himself in protest after authorities took away his last effort to feed his family decently. Tunisia erupted and has since been inching toward normalcy in hopes of a new utopia as Ben Ali, the former Tunisian president fled the country to Saudi Arabia. The Domino effect moved to Egypt, Libya, Yemen, Bahrain and Syria.

In Egypt, and though the bar was set quite high by the Pharos, today's Egyptians lived up to the legacy and sent President Mubarak to the gallows. Incredible as it seems in one surreal scene and as thousands of demonstrators packed the famous Tahrir Square, a 7th century jockey shows up on his camel to disperse the crowd with a whipping frenzy. As the crowds drag and maul the crazy rider, how, who and where from remain a puzzle for documentary writers.

People governing themselves proved to be a tough business to achieve quickly following the long President Mubarak rule, and for now the military in Egypt continues to run the show and the public is still in limbo on whether they plan to let go. With opposition led by splintered factions and groups following the euphoric Revolution, it does not create a monolithic front and the power to remove all the old regime point men, much less the military and establishment henchmen.

At the south entrance to the Red Sea, NATO warships and the pirates from Africa are still in a game of cat-and-mouse on how to maximize their own share of commerce. As NATO forces try to protect shipping lanes for trade convoys, the pirates expanded their reach all through the Indian Ocean and towards the Arabian Sea, an area so large that even the whales get lost at sea. Pirates are not making the headlines anymore but can be found in the back pages of the news.

At that bottleneck, Yemen is there, real strategic, has been and will always be. No wonder they originated languages and religions and much of the history of old of the Arab world. Their on-going revolution remains a work in progress, women leading the charge much of the time demanding accountability of the regime for decades of alleged crimes.

In Morocco, the King wisely ceded some power and called for elections, giving the people ample changes to have more democracy. Jordan experienced some tension, the King there moving rapidly to absorb it and respond to public demands. Jordan is not in control of its future, and sits sandwiched between friend and foe, uncertain which is which while waiting for clouds to clear up and for prosperity to flow.

In Syria, an uprising has been going on for nine months, and so far the government seems still in control with very little split within the military, a catalyst which was banked on for toppling the regime. Referred to by various networks as a revolution, the timing is similar to events before in Iraq's invasion in 2003 when Saddam Hussein had already negotiated oil contracts with Russia, France and Germany. Syria's gas contracts were negotiated with Russia and China and the West was left out. Same in Libya, the Italian energy powerhouse ENI and Russia had secured vast privileges from Qaddafi to pump the highly refined oil.

Syria is at the super powers crossroads, and at the intersection of global interests and a land gateway to the region and its energy resources. It's a high stakes conflict, East and West. For one side a change to a friendlier regime was deemed possible while for the other keeping the status go was more plausible. For now it seems at a standstill, but for Turkey it may already be overtime.

Turkey had more projects in Syria than has any other country with a positive balance of over one billion dollars. Though significant, it pales when compared to Turkey's export market to the United Arab Emirates of over eight billion dollars. Turkey's Prime Minister Erdogan took a stand against Syria calling for sanctions, only later to face the reality that much of Turkey's trade to the rest of the Arab World passes through Syria. He may be on thin ice with the Turkish public come election time as his aggressive stance against the Syrian regime is hurting Turkey's private business interests, and the street is not happy about a tense situation with unforeseen consequences at best.

To understand more about the region, we may need to revisit a music symphony by one of Italy's most famous composers of the early 1900's, Giuseppe Verdi. Named Nabucco, it recounts the story of Nebuchadnezzar, the king of Babylon who uprooted many Jews and brought them to his empire some 2500 years ago. The political plot thickens when Nabucco becomes the name of the proposed pipeline to carry gas from Azerbaijan all the way to Europe via Turkey in order to reduce the total gas reliance of Europe on Gazprom, the giant Russian oil company. In due course the newly found gas in the Mediterranean across the coasts of Israel, Lebanon, Syria and Cyprus is to connect with Nabucco. The pipeline would have bypassed Greece in favor of Turkey to receive the transportation royalties, a carrot to get Prime Minister

Erdogan on board to aggressively advocate change in Syria. So far Verdi's Nabucco is alive and well, let's all hope this reconfigured symphony ends up well.

As a world class scramble is underway by superpowers and various countries to participate in the East Mediterranean gas, Brazil sent a frigate to the region, and Russia which lost of much of its influence in former European and Arab countries also sent navy ships to the Syrian coast. Together with China, their veto is controlling the outcome from the UN. In lieu of the Axis versus the Allies during the last two world wars, and with Brazil, Russia, India and China as main players this time, could it be the BRICS versus the Allies in an upcoming Third World War?

In the broader scope, would revolutions take place if the population had the right to bear arms as in the United States? Will there be vigilantes when living and dying come face to face on either side of the armed divide? The verdict is still out as we conclude this year and the Crystal Ball must go out before the end of the year.

Many are voicing threats of a strike against nuclear installations in Iran. Though such an action has been flaunted numerous times, there are unfathomed consequences of what may happen with a nuclear cloud moving over the continent, and the potential destabilization of oil with the closure of the Strait of Hormuz or the flaming of the Gulf region oil facilities. If all else fails, the nuclear club may consider future coexistence with a nuclear Iran in the hope that in time a friendly government will become in charge.

Dormant for almost what seemed like eternity, the

Arab league awakened recently and joined the fray, shuttling politicos across Arab capitals and international centers of world power. Another change is on the scene, the Palestinian Authority was voted in as a member of the UNESCO against the wishes of the US and Israel. Bolstered with much unrest around it, Israel enjoys a relative peace while it populates lands around Jerusalem with new settlements under the Biblical.

Lebanon has been at peace with the current caretaker government, on the sidelines for now watching the unfolding of events all across the region. It's such a beautiful country and enterprising people with no limits on creativity and optimism towards a bright future. By some statistics, around sixty percent of the students there attend private schools, an incredible percentage and the source of so much flex in ideas and languages, and the capacity to capture emerging trends from other cultures and retool them with so much versatility.

The prospects for peace in the Middle East next year are slim since there are many countries in turmoil and a peace is an Israel / Palestine is only a piece of the overall peace. What gets not talked about is the impact of a Middle East peace on the surrounding countries and various sparring entities.

Can the Palestinians continue to have Hamas and the PLO in two separate entities in a dispute? Could this be a smart approach to prevent total capitulation, and to maintain options on how to form the new nation? Could Hezbollah in Lebanon be very keen on keeping Lebanon whole as an act of self-preservation to forestall Israeli raids if Lebanon is split into religious reservations?

Can Israel survive its internal political, ethnic and religious divisions and splintered parties without a continuous external threat? How to keep internal harmony and peace may prove as challenging as achieving the much sought after Arab-Israeli peace.

A closure of sorts took place earlier this year as Osama Bin laden was finally taken out in a sophisticated operation that was years in the making. In a strange twist of fate, a US military plane carrying navy seals went down in Afghanistan not too long thereafter, leading many to try and connect the dots in such a remote region and sort the disaster. North Korea continues the ruling dynasty with the son taking charge after the passing of his father, fulfilling the dream of the original founder of the dynasty, his grandfather. In a different way, Mexico is struggling against the powerful drug lords newly established dynasty, a survival game between money and arms versus morals and poverty.

Through it all, the future shows signs that are positive and optimistic for the relatively cash liquid Middle East while much of Europe is in a fix with high debt and much unrest, and which brings us back full circle to Greece, hovering and teetering on the edge of the precipice. European Stock markets shuddered every time Greece offered sovereign bonds for sale and the rates kept climbing. A default by Greece will drag the Euro down and shatter the Euro Club peace. The debt of Greece, Portugal, Spain and Italy is overshadowing all the good news and Europe could implode on itself under the huge sovereign debt blues.

Europe's problems were compounded by many labor strikes affecting public transportation and travel. There were street blockades in Greece, London's Heathrow airport was shut down for a day, and many world subways where vulnerable for days. The damage adds up and the impact becomes long lasting as world travelers begin to avoid potential bottlenecks and skip cities known for active labor protests. In the showdown between the challengers of free market capitalism the innocent traveler will simply choose alternative carriers for reliable transportation to an altogether different destination.

Forward again, the world is moving into spheres of influence. There was a time when it was much easier to have a world with 2 to 3 empires and with fewer countries as the rulers controlled all the land and assets. Today Australia is more connected by trade to the Far East than to its original European heritage. With globalization a number of large countries disintegrated including Yugoslavia, the Soviet Union and Sudan which split itself into two.

The future is in flex for large countries with a multitude of ethnicities and languages such as India and China. There are undercurrents to have more of the small and less of the large as the latter may pose an existential threat to others. At the other extreme new virtual nations are formed with no territory and with multiple nationalities, and their lands are Four Seasons and other star studded hotels. The super rich may not need a country as they jet set from country to country.

In any case holding a large country together is becoming a real challenge for the rulers and democracy is facing the test of proving its worth long term. Democracy in small countries falls back to religious sects as they become the political parties and divisions run along ethnic and religious lines. Real democracy requires large countries in order to dilute religion into more important but mundane aspects such as jobs and the economy. In poorer countries Democracy takes a back seat to survival, as Maslow's famous Hierarchy of Needs remains stronger than ethics and sticking to good deeds. In advanced democracies candidates solicit campaign funds but in poor ones they dole out funds and privileges as part of the rich class to woo the votes from the underprivileged class.

A democracy of sorts is taking roots in China as the size gets too large for centralized governing and power needs to be transferred to the local authorities for most matters. A real fear is haunting the financial markets as to where the economy of China is headed, and for some outside powers a long term policy is to have a splintered China or several mini-Chinas. The Dalai Llama gets ample support and limelight so far in the media in hopes of a separate Tibet run from the palaces of the historic capital, Lhasa. Some reports on China suggest a very high inflation rate while the private sector share of GDP is below par. The economy may be on the verge of a recession, government spending on infrastructure and new cities is way up, and overall taxes are among the highest in the world. Some suggest China may be in a deep hole with billions in interest payments.

The US Economy is facing its own problems with the national debt: the billion made a reverse split and became a trillion, and the numbers range from 4 to 14 to 114 trillion in unfunded liabilities. Congress will not set a committee to find where the trillions were spent as many politicians accept the national debt increase versus the potential social unrest if there is no money flowing to the people.

According to some the U.S. has the second highest corporate tax rate in the world, leaving us to ponder which country is first. The rate along with high labor costs forced many companies to go overseas, whether to Southeast Asia or South America, and as capital is all over the board it is more reason for the US to have a strong military to protect investments abroad. The US has done well recycling petrodollars since oil producing countries buy back in return oil equipment, and military hardware and planes feeding production and employment.

One can only wonder what would have been the state of the US economy and much of the West if the bulk of Oil underground was in countries such as China and India that have more appetite for the black gold and may not be willing to share, and there would be no petrodollars to repatriate but simply more debt. The friendly oil producing countries in the Arab World and elsewhere can be seen in a different light and with less maligning in the media considering what would have the alternative to such an accident of earth geology.

Small countries such as Kuwait, Qatar and the United Arab Emirates built great airlines with hundreds of planes crisscrossing continents when they could have remained relying on foreign carriers from all over and simply stashed the petrodollars for a future rainy day. Such ventures changed the dynamics of travel as transcontinental travelers on Qatar Airways and Emirates bypass Europe's airports on their way to the Middle East and Southeast Asia, and Europe is missing out big in on the lucrative transatlantic world travel.

Being small and rich some petro countries end up with a low citizen population versus high foreign workers. With globalization, how long will this imbalance continue into the future as nationhood becomes unrelated to language, ethnic make-up or religion? Can capitalism become the common bond and will it succeed at building pluralistic states?

The price of oil has been reasonably steady for much of the year even with the revolution in Libya and troubles in Bahrain. Crude in tankers used as floating storage has been consumed and there is no glut in sight. We may have gotten used the price of barrel around $100 give or take, but any jolt can have drastic results. Louisiana is always on alert as to when they may need to open the flood gates to the spillway built in 1954 to release the waters of the mighty Mississippi river, and as luck would have it, the Colonial Oil Pipeline which feeds 12 states is located in the same flood plain and is always at risk of damage or possibly floating altogether, sending both oil and its price skywards.

The new proposed pipeline from Canada to Houston refineries faces the typical environmental dilemma and delays from various politicos hyping their electorate by putting the screws under the guise of saving nature and preventing eco-systems abuse.

A new gold coin was minted in Australia, over one ton of pure stuff worth over 50 million dollars before gold collapsed towards the end of this year due to a rally in the dollar. Gold demand has seasons based on the annual celebrations in some countries where gold is used for jewelry. In China gold for jewelry exceeds demand for bullion and so it is with India, to a point where global demand for jewelry is over 50% of industrial demand, and nearly 2/3 of the total demand is from central banks. Keep an eye on the size of ear rings and necklaces to gage the price direction and take stock.

Inflation continues to simmer unnoticed and hidden from the daily news. It is easier on the public this way, less stress about the future. Which brings us to stocks: how to handle the bull going bare, when the bear already gobbled up the feedstock to buy stocks with no reserves to spare?

To figure it out, buy, sell or hold, the Lunar Calendar is getting more religiously followed, not by the faithful and believers but by Wall Street gurus who figured out the strange relationship between market tops on the charts and the full moon, and market bottoms at the start of a new moon. The Lord may have sent the signal long ago with the lunar orbit suggesting the markets flux with the low and high tides, maybe sublime signals for trading charts.

For more clues on leading edge indicators on market direction check companies which make locomotives parts and freight cars, the shipping index and large office furniture makers. As large companies and government hire after downsizing in a recession, they need new furniture and cubicle stations.

The Crystal Ball offers another hint on a real and sensitive indicator that can guide the way, though it may be hard for ladies to closely check its accuracy. For astute men aficionados, the method to measure economic activity is to track the sale of men's underwear starting with one's self: constant in normal times, the sales drop in recessions as men have less money to spare and get tight about spending for underwear.

Back in the US, the "Occupy Wall Street" movement is asking for a share of the dream. They turned Wall Street into a fort sheltering Wall Street insiders, by now hedging with bailout Futures against a full assault on the Street. Some authorities acted as if they are dealing with barbarians at the gate, when they're the real world acting in faith and trying to limit future "finance-gates". The movement raises questions about the future of parks and large squares of our cities in terms of security as crowds converge on them in times of dissent and could paralyze daily life.

At the University of Houston and following the demonstrations in the late sixties against the Vietnam War in the large field adjacent to the University Center, the square was dug-up, a large underground of facilities was built and the square became a series of pathways between various structures. Could this be the future of our squares and parks? Will parks

become peripheral suburban locations where demonstrators could camp for days and weeks without
being noticed if the media shuts out the objective and
fair voices? Do we build future parks as forts?

Calling for change just as President Obama pro-
claimed when he was a candidate, Republicans want
a total administration change. Since about midyear,
the talk of the media pundits is about republican
presidential hopefuls ahead of US presidential elections next year. The roster includes a wide range of
ideologues, it is too late for new entrants, and the
debates are consuming the candidates: confronta-
tions, scandals, immigration and border security,
pensions and the budget, jobs, and deficits and taxes.
Candidates have become unpaid actors filling the
print media and TV time at a fraction of the normal
cost of regular programs, and with more income
generated by the constant unsavory ads about how
to empower the testosterone drive and renew happiness between partners, and the tasteless hounding
about effective urinary tract medicine at lunch and
dinner, and even at breakfast.

Last year the Crystal Ball predicted that Governor
Perry of Texas has powerful credentials to enter the
presidential race. This year he did though late, and
was playing catch up with other candidates who had
been already drilled and more seasoned. Though the
gaff about the 3rd one that Perry could not remember
haunted him for a while, his credentials as Governor
for 11 years of a State the size of France remains formidable and he has a rich war chest to keep the fight.
It is a long campaign till the summer of 2012 and the

Republican convention, money counts and only candidates with a large war chest can continue the quest
to wear the presidential vest.

Taxing the rich is always a provocative topic and
the stuff of much debate. Many of the rich receive
capital gains and unearned income in lieu of regular
income and are taxed differently altogether. The
Crystal Ball cautions against more income tax as it
becomes detrimental to purchasing power by a 10 to
20 multiplier effect, because it reduces the leverage
of the individual when making large purchases. A
person with a $150,000 income can get a mortgage
on a home for 500,000 but an additional tax of five
percent or $7,500 reduces the ability to purchase by
$100,000 to $200,000 depending on the rate of interest.
This applies to all brackets, and the lower the income,
the higher the effect is on purchasing ability because
of credit sensitivity. Though some consider it a small
tax increment, the downward leverage aspect with
the multiplier is drastic and it will take the longer to
move the inventory of foreclosed homes.

Jobs, jobs and more jobs are the answer but it
will to take a long time before we can come close to
full employment again. Advanced manufacturing
requires less people, and the coveted 4.5% unemployment rate is now a dream as entrants to the
labor force from graduations, immigration and the
previously unemployed appear beyond the present
system capacity with all the national debt which is
compounding larger daily.

On the happy social front, the year was enchanted
by royal news with the wedding of Prince Williams

and Kate Middleton in British style and pageantry and all the preceding and follow-up bits and tips from socialites and promoters of royalty. On another front with underground news, the publishing empire of Rupert Murdock came under fire this year, with allegations that sensational stories were obtained by tapping phones of the rich and famous, and the notorious. The empire rarely publishes on its own story, and we're beginning to forget the whole story.

The host of Larry King Live bowed out this year, leaving one of our favorite nightly programs in a state of flux as the new host Piers Morgan remains in the making and explores all avenues and packs the show with star studded guests to recapture the old master of the game ratings. And after twenty five years of The Oprah Winfrey Show, Oprah is taking a deserved break until she figures the next perennial TV show.

Global warming is staring its arch enemy global cooling face to face: which way out, up or down. Debate continues with both sides hardening their positions on Green. Ice cores take us back some 700,000 years to check temperature. More CO_2 in the atmosphere may be the cause of faster growth of plants as they feed on carbon, and records show that CO_2 was much higher during the dinosaurs' era, fueling speculation on whether humans will become dinosaurously taller and larger with more global warming in our future.

Saving energy and sustaining earth is our responsibility. In lieu of cutting trees, maybe we can do the logging in rivers underwater and pull out already submerged trees whether due to dams or simply the natural cycle. Solar could still be viable given the right technology, and plenty of sun. As the oil era recedes, will future wars be about areas with uninterrupted year-round sun or continuous steady 24 hours a day winds?

A couple more energy saving tips: growing marijuana indoors to hide from sky eyes consumes one percent of electricity. Moving the plants outdoors saves much energy and gives an environmental leg to legalization advocates in their drug liberation quest. In Japan, it turns out personal hygiene one button clean-us-up toilets which sprays and dries us effortlessly and pioneered by Toto consume four percent of household electricity. Expect a national strike if it comes to a "Totoesque" electricity saving ban.

Our earth/space satellites partnership which gave us the present Global Positioning System (GPS) is about to get more precise with the use of four satellites in lieu of three to locate us wherever we are within few feet if not inches. No way out of this one and no place to run unless you switch off all electronics and live back like a cave man.

Particle Colliders are making news, with CERN's large Hadron collider near Geneva putting on display extraterrestrial speed. A rival, the Fermi National Accelerator Laboratory, claims to have found a Higgs boson, the missing link in subatomic science. Another unfathomed particle, the neutrino, should be so abundant in space but is so hard to detect. According to some, a beam of neutrinos could be used to penetrate stellar space and communicate with aliens, if they are out there waiting for a hello from us homo-sapiens. Scientists are also convinced there is dark matter so stay on the lookout for who may be hiding in that dark before sunrise, science can still surprise.

The String Theory continues to gain momentum as a likely explanation of the universe, how it started, and whether there are several universes out there or a multiverse as it is referred to. The problem that haunts this theory relates to the need mathematically for ten spatial dimensions, some say eleven in lieu of the known three. Doubters have a hard time how to visualize such dimensions, especially when some are at the invisible Nano level. Since Time is sometimes referred to as the fourth dimension, The Crystal Ball can suggest a few more dimensions such as sound, color, vision and the sixth sense.

As part of this universe, we are galactic subjects riding the space waves round and round and sub-jected to the same magnetic forces that affect birds and other animals and make them react ahead of nature's acts. How do these solar and other extra-terrestrial cycles affect us as humans and can we revive the evolutionary bird ancestry within our minds to get the same sense of direction and upcoming dangers?

From the not so far outer space, the Moon with its elliptical orbit is a magnet for enchantment and night lovers: is it an innocent bystander, or is it compound-ing the effects of the magnetic system when it reacts to different cosmic radiations? Some scientists have correlated this activity and believe it can give signals on upcoming seismic activity and earthquakes.

Whenever talk is about space, it is befitting to

look at Religion. Nothing is sacred nowadays, not even the private confessions to the priest behind the veiled cloth of the Roman Catholic Church. Confessions can now be done by touching the screen of the I-pad once you download the new divine wonder: I-Confess App.

Every year we check on rare metals since their stocks soar sometimes, much to our regret and chagrin almost always when we're sidelined. With the growing demand for hybrid and electric vehicles demand for rare earths intensifies, especially as current battery power for cars is short on long distance yet long on shear weight, and costs are on the increase to develop enough energy storage versus the miles to travel without the excessive batteries heavy weight.

Enter thermoelectric generation, a new and promising energy if only the right rare metal is produced and in enough quantities. Last year we reviewed Coltan, difficult to mine as it is present in areas of Africa where Gorillas reside. As luck would have it, our desired rare metal this year is produced near Wild Bears in cold mines of Norway. Known as Skutterudite, it is an arsenic mineral of the Cobalt family, and with the right technology it can convert heat into kilowatt power. It is near a scramble now as auto makers are in a race not to be left out, and to be first in getting their thermo cars out.

Rare metals remain easier to find than individual stars, and this year we lost a superstar of our times and maybe of all times, Apple's founder Steve Jobs. With creativity, determination, willpower and incredible vision, Steve Jobs created the Mac, the Graphical Interface, the Mouse, and Airport Extreme to connect to the internet. Beyond IPod and the I-Phone, Jobs succeeded at maximizing Apple as a company and assembled the right management to create huge profits and advance science. One of the best companies in the world, the brand is everywhere and global and his legacy is bound to be generational.

In the world of Smoke, the black market for cigars from Cuba is thriving and well, as the tasty smoke is distributed illegally worldwide since the Cuban government nationalized that industry in 1959. Though the price is premium, it is low in relation to the desired high and the ultimate satisfaction from puffing to blow smoke in the face of the agents of the crackdown.

This year we had significant travels to many faraway destinations. Our world is a fascinating place and people are a lot closer to each other than they think. As Singapore Air stops in Moscow I had a chance to tour Red Square, the Kremlin, and several neighborhoods and museums well stocked with masterpieces by Monet and Chagall and many famous artists brought back to Moscow during the dominance years. Memories came back of a time when we grew up surrounded by Capitalism, Communism, Socialism, and Maoism, all vying for our attention in turbulent times. Though it was closed for remodeling at the time, the Bolshoi Theater still stands imposing on its own square and reopened thereafter, a compelling reason to come back to Moscow for this one of a kind experience next season.

From Moscow to Singapore, flying above Afghan-istan at night is an eerie feeling as one searches in vain for remnants of new Marco Polos' on The Silk Road that once was there. There are long stretches of total darkness over the mountain chains, and as the plane passes between the lights of Kabul and Kandahar, one is reminded that there is war simmer-ing down there and wonders what are the chances a rogue missile may hit the plane. A serene feeling takes over once the plane is over the Indian Ocean, although flying over any water at night carries its own sense of surrendering to one's own fate and by then it is too late.

The Marina Bay hotel complex in Singapore with the large penthouse infinity pool is a masterpiece on its own, overlooking the modern downtown and one of the busiest ports in the world where hundreds of ships pass by daily. Driving on the left there needs getting used to. It is an old tradition mainly to keep the horse whip away from the sidewalk as most people are right handed and allows one to carry a sword or weapon on the side of a potential oncoming threat. France's emperor Napoleon is credited with the change as he was left handed.

A Kuala Lumpur visit was a must to pay homage to the PETRONAS Towers, incredible buildings from every angle with a superb multilevel mall stretching out. Lightening protection for such metallic build-ings is a real feat as repeated lightening strikes the two buildings at night with high intensity to give the locals an awesome spectacle of the clash between metal and electricity.

There is a gigantic Times Square in Kuala Lumpur, the Berjaya Times Square, world class twin towers 48 stories each with more than 1,000 retail shops and 1200 luxury hotel suites, a powerful shopping magnet in sheer size of space. The city's monorail stops in front high up on level 4 and shopping is in two ten story atriums connected by a disneyesque play land where the train rides up several floors and then comes tumbling down in the huge air-conditioned space, the largest indoor theme park in Asia. When heat and humidity are coupled with capital and foresight, they can really change urban concepts with forward vision and progressive insight.

Sydney is a shining metropolis rich with the contributions of its diverse and enterprising communities. The Opera House is so grand and striking at first sight, a meeting of the minds between nature and architecture and a great world heritage site. Public transport is excellent and efficient and becomes an unforgettable journey since the nearly four dollars fare for the shortest bus trip sticks to your memory. Istanbul was my first time and it is simply phenomenal. I got to see the mosques and buildings I studied at Architecture School and heard about all my life: Topkapi, Hagia Sofia, The Blue Mosque, and the Sulaimaniyeh Mosque which tops all. Just like other empires throughout the times, the Ottomans brought back precious artifacts from faraway lands, including Prophet Mohammad's clothes and swords on display in a special museum section of Topkapi. For great pastime, it is bargaining at the grand indoor bazaar.

Worldwide population is on the increase and

tourists are multiplying everywhere creating long lines and bottlenecks at all significant world sites. The future is also challenging Architecture as millions live in unacceptable conditions. How to build an affordable livable house at a fraction of today's costs to allow equity build up for many to pull out of poverty? Can we build a neighborhood with these homes? With high property taxes and unattainable credit for many, will they be fixed or on wheels, or floating structures on rivers and lakes? Indeed one of the great future challenges of society.

In Texas we had a record drought this year and lost hundreds of thousands of trees, some in our own yard, and wild fires engulfed large areas in many counties. Nature has a way of reminding us periodically of how little control we have on our lives and how expensive it is to remove the remnants of one of her trees when we have to pay for it ourselves. Nature's advice: Don't Mess With Texas…

US space travel is grinding to a halt victim of budget cuts as our future and science lost this fight, and we bid farewell to the U.S. Space Shuttle Discovery as it made its final landing, altogether thirty nine incredible flights.

Life is a high stakes game and we get to play. Enjoy the game including the highs and the lows as risk and reward change over time. We cannot live back in time when the future itself cannot catch up with the speed of our advancing times. Reflecting on our lives and looking forward is a challenging task that forces one to reach within for outlook and understanding of the world and life altogether. Accidents of History are not predictable but with vision, perseverance and style, and observations and astute analysis, we may achieve successful forecasting. Let each of us do visioning and review from our own point of view, read the signals of our Crystal ball and do right to set the example and to benefit those around us with the right clues.

Happy Holidays, and until next year
Imad F. Abdullah, December 2011

The Year 2010

2010 HAS BEEN THE YEAR earth totally lost its cool, getting fed up with us humans taking for granted her selfless bounty and continuously abusing her largesse and generosity.

When earth packs heat, it reminds us of how precarious our existence can be on this planet. Earth asserted its will and blew its top ferociously over Iceland, the volcano spreading ash to fill the skies and blanket all the land. The continent of Europe was held hostage for days as planes were unable to fly inside the thick ash haze, and together with the year-end ice storms, they turned airports into gargantuan hotels stranding passengers in a nightmarish daze. Earth sent a quake to Chile, flooded Pakistan and China, and earlier in the year, Haiti was literally wasted by "The Earthquake". Streets and buildings twisted with violent shakes, and in due course Haiti succumbed to famine and a mean Cholera outbreak.

Fires lit up Portugal, Russia and California as if to balance all ends of the planet. Today's fire season is 78 days longer than 30 years ago, and still more fires in

Indonesia are manmade to clear land into farmland, before a proposed government moratorium becomes law of the land.

On everyone's mind, the war in Afghanistan simmers to no end, as a new General is sent to test the latest strategic trends, and the media is toning down reporting to calm the public with a fake pretend. The war may appear close to an end but can there really be an end?

Iran continues to claim its share of political fame, missiles and the nuclear always newsworthy and a national pride claim. The newly re-elected President Ahmadinejad is basking in the limelight, and tripping to various capitals for friends and allies. Darfur is next though now standing aside, while the south of Sudan awaits the divide. Iraq is in a Government checkers game, and the Mexican warlords are carrying a horrendously indifferent game.

N Korea wants to be in the news. When it is not covered prime, it takes matters in its own hand and makes waves with a big bang. China cannot afford for a communist neighboring regime to collapse, the Koreas tit for tat a minuscule game of cat and mouse. The real scare is if North and South reunite to become one giant with formidable industry, similar to the powerhouse of the united East and West Germany. The stakes continue to get higher in the Far-East, as to who survives and who can still compete.

China continues on its meteoric rise, propelled by the wonderland 2010 World's Fair in Shanghai, a city anticipated to grow from 19 to 45 millions in 2025. Disneyland is in "depeche mode" to open there,

Volvo's hot, and the humming "Hummer" is boosting China's surplus trade. At a dizzying speed, China has become the world's laboratory for future experimentation, as science intensifies the race towards the always fictitious edge, and pushes the envelope to catch with the ever expanding knowledge.

Being in the center of a tumultuous region and at the crossroads of continents has its benefits. The growth of Turkey is surpassed only by China and India, and all 3 countries have an enviable population growth. The shuttle back and forth to the Middle East was full all year, talks are on and off again, and the ultimate peace is still undisturbed and resting in peace. Israel spent the last two years in preparation for the future negotiations of a contemplated peace, and profited handsomely from continuing the talks as the US offered them and their counterpart Palestinian negotiators a sweet deal. Can there be peacemaking without future bribes, and will the historic legacy of the peacemakers transcend how and what to divide?

Though there are countries around the globe with a multitude of religions, Lebanon is an experiment in what happens when various factions do not control their own actions. Lebanese circles encircle their inner circles, wrap their perennial political candidates with the loyalty to faith and Party, and surround their upstarts with the same ideology. Can Lebanon rise to the opportunity to develop collective religions into a model government form, and contribute the magic formula to the world to become the norm?

Worldwide, religions continue to agree on the mundane and the real, and disagree on the supernatural and the surreal. Religion has always been at odds with science, and as archaeology continues to dig under, religion works to advance the mind through the beyond to the eternal wonder. With no peer review for their medicine or tests, religions promise happiness through eternal salvation to the faithful of all sects.

The future of wars is undergoing extensive research as all types of arsenals have been tried so far, unable still to get it right whether conflicts are near or afar. For now super powers impose embargoes and restrictions as a substitute for invasions, but the "embargoed" are stocking missiles and hyping nuclear fears, and some retaliate as pirates on the high seas. New methods may soon be found as sensors could become the new army robots in the field, fighting in lieu of soldiers as small dust particles, blanketing the enemy into chilled surrender with their infinitesimal obstacles. The war on terror remains of a different tune, creating lots of jobs for unscrupulous contractors hiring hungry soldiers of fortune.

Some talk radio and few other TV channels fill the airtime with repetitive tidbits and soap highlights, rounding free actors among politicians looking for exposure and a chance to get some limelight. Beyond orphan politics all day pumped up as news, nature's disasters puncture the routine every now and then with breaking news. The attention span is getting short, and to treat the national attention deficit syndrome, we get continuous hounding to "keep them honest" popping on TV screens in our homes.

Back to finance where money gives us a cheer, borrowing power is now the new frontier. Capitalism is moving ahead faster of government in democracies, yet is getting behind in totalitarian regimes and Autocracy. As wars create instability and uncertainty, they prevent countries from creating capital or raising money. The world straddles 2 camps, those who can print money and borrow selling bonds, and those who operate on a cash basis and ponder how to reach the prosperity pond. The Euro is getting riskier as Greece teeters and Spain shivers, Ireland is trapped within and Portugal is on edge, and France is in limbo as baby boomers and the older generation battle the 62 years retirement age.

The Sterling is living up to its sterling reputation as the UK watches the debt assault on the Euro next door. The EU is on the hook, leaning on Germany to shore up the Euro, but a Europe once famous for its wars could be on the verge of a big debt bout, which members stay Euro and who gets booted out. How many countries can the EU bail out before Germany decides to find its own way-out? Will the EU disintegrate and go broke, and who will come to the rescue once the clock on the Euro runs out?

Third World status may reach the Alps if countries in Southern Europe fail to make the cut. The Crystal Ball suggests empowering more women, as economies have proven more successful when their involvement gets as high as men. And just in case systems fail, the Economics of Poverty is a whole new field where the existing models are out of their league. Forget Margin reserves, capital flow, Swift, and fine-tuning: the poor are producers and consumers with a whole set of requirements and strategy, and unless given a different try, the master mechanics from Harvard Economics need not apply.

Oil has been dancing around all year, supplies plentiful with the underground storage in Oklahoma and other salt domes near capacity with no shortage to fear. Peter and his Principle continue to challenge our ingenuity, as the BP Maconda well safety redundancy tried to call his bluff but failed miserably. In the Gulf of Mexico, where normally750,000 barrels seep into the water every year which industry is unable to stop, Offshore drilling came to a halt when the notorious well blew its Christmas Tree top. For a while water became thick black paste, the nightmarish oil spill turning marine life into waste. Miraculously, earth rejuvenated itself by feeding oil to bacteria and fish life, giving the crude industry a whole new lease on life. Though Angola is sitting on 13 billion barrels still waiting for political stability, Oil will remain for the distant future in our destiny, as solar power remains at the mercy of the government subsidy.

Wind power may have a larger role in our future. As we battle the global warming trend, we may need to reverse the blades into giant cooling fans across the globe from end to end. In a different twist and befitting the location on the Italian island of Sicily, somewhere near Palermo, subsidies of the wind turbines generated so much money to the locals even though the prevailing winds have not lived up to their touted strength and intensity. To make sure the cash flow continues, rumor has it the savvy "Palermosi" secretly built hidden diesel generators to produce electricity, the grid connected to the wind turbines to show benefactors the success of the enterprise and to continue the cash flow from "renewable energy".

Money from lenders has been very scarce yet so cheap, flying in the face of established theories of supply and demand as banks keep piling and topping their cash heap. Inflation has been double-faced this year, hovering near zero in public, but rising steadily behind the scene. High inflation is good for paying debt with lower value dollars from the State, bad for deficits as interest rates rise to compensate. The Fed is now printing so much that it has to print a whole lot more to buy the instruments it issues and sells at the treasury auctions. As public debt soars, is there a limit before the collapse?

Estimates are that public debt can reach an absolute limit at 160% of Gross Domestic Product, after which the "Down" begins spiraling. Though the Dollar has steadily declined, it remains the currency of choice for large holdings. US Bonds have been selling well at near zero coupons to park cash in safe instruments, and the US is on safe grounds for future borrowing as demand could outstrip the printing press if bonds offer two to three percent higher rates. They would still be extremely low by historical standards, especially when compared to the eighteen percent interest rates only thirty years hence when President Carter left office.

Our national debt never had it so good, now

strapping every American to the hilt, their kids and kids of kids. Our cash is at a loss where to park itself, chasing fractions of a point between money market accounts, and the short and long term CD's and bonds are subject to interest tricks, uncertain as the principal drops with each rate up tick. Few can assume the risk of downward leverage with rates near zero and are staying put, and though it may sound stupid, the downside from zero is actually the potential drop of the asset acquired by the cash in treacherous markets. A new facet is entering economics: Decumulation of Assets.

Now near the end of his second year, President Obama can't escape but own-up to all his predecessor problems over those 8 Republican years. Presidential legacies were mainly self- made, but they are sometimes reconstructed, just as President "W" Bush did with his Memoirs recently published. President Obama's legacy is somewhat out of hand for now, pending nature's mercy with the oil spill and the potential default on sovereign debt. Hot on the jobless, America's researchers always astound us with inordinate statistics, some suggest that 1/3 of our GDP (Gross Development Product) is spent correcting mistakes, a dire legacy omen for improving productivity and unemployment rates.

The "Jobs Deck" is constantly shuffled for the unemployed and the underemployed. In the early stages of an upturn, and when hiring starts, more unemployed rejoin the search. The lag between rising vacancies and falling unemployment keeps the rates difficult to predict. With interest rates near zero and only marginal growth the last 2 years, the Fed is in a tough spot on how to spur growth by shifting to lower rate gears. To compound the effect, the new generation, half the size of the older is in a race, and may pay double taxes just to keep pace.

President Obama's own implied pledge of "read my lips" is not working with the tax bill, just as it haunted the elder President Bush in his quest for a failed second term to recapture control over the hill. Spreading the wealth is heavily contested by the wealthy, and Republicans want to reduce Democrats dependency. The results of the midterm congressional elections changed the make-up structure, too much political capital invested on the Healthcare Bill as resentment grew at every juncture. Now comes Wikipedia and Wickileaks, and we're just beginning to flip through that new American Chapter, the internet face to face with the Establishment and its power structure.

The former White House Chief of Staff Rahm Emmanuel resigned to run for Mayor of Chicago, the signals and vibes not lost on the insiders on why to abandon ship and such a sensitive post, to try for an office with a lot less oomph to boast. Was it failure on the job or lack of loyalty, or just a personal career change before the Obama administration becomes toast?

Illegal migration to the US remains a hot potato, Congress and everyone except Arizona still in limbo. The immigration process has always been hampered by the starved funding of the Agency, under the guise of "shortage of money". Ironically when the financial system was about to implode, a trillion Dollars was invented out of thin air for Banks to reload. Would we have 10 million or more staying illegally, had their papers been processed over the years in a timely manner by a well-funded agency?

Positioning for president is only for the hardy and not an easy feat, but former Alaska Governor Sara Palin is laughing happy as she amasses millions in fees and film royalty, teasing everyone on whether she'll be the 2012 candidate for the Republican Party. The quest requires too many advisers, expect an internal gridlock before she gets everyone on board and ready, as the pundits will be in line to bring her to reality.

The stock markets performed reasonably well in 2010, and if you missed the ride hop on board for 2011. In the third year of a presidency the famed Dow Jones has an astounding statistic, up 95% of the time. Instant Information and insider tips for everyone can be too late and useless when it comes to trading stocks, as such needs insight and the skill to execute and ensure profits get locked. The key denominator to trading is now execution speed, thousands of trades per second, with the NASDAQ working at 177 microseconds. The markets are quite alive as companies sell to emerging countries worldwide, and the stock values are back from their lows just in time to give us a cheer and a big holiday glow.

A lot of real estate remains upside down, topside heavy, underwater, and non-performing. Foreclosures are still rampant, and the economy cannot afford the coveted six percent returns without high risk instruments. Though gold looks strong and shinier than ever, trading is riskier as the bullion is bought in cash or as Exchange Traded Funds, and requires investors with strong guts to stomach the daily gyrations of their funds.

Rare metals are more frequent in the news, as they are used in present and some still futuristic discoveries. Last year The Crystal Ball highlighted Neodymium, a component of strong permanent magnets. This year the focus is on Coltan, shortened by industry for Columbo-Tantalite, the source of Tantalum, an invaluable metal in many hi-tech and medical applications due to its strength, chemistry and electronic properties. Foremost, it is a backbone to our beloved cell phones. America is no longer a great mining nation but as luck would have it, rare metals are spread in many exotic places, such as deep in Mongolia where the gigantic statue of Genghis Khan on his horse guards the new airport, a stark reminder of past glory of an endless empire. More challenging, Coltan is mined from deep in the jungles of the Congo where it shares the land with our primate ancestors, Gorillas. Needless to say, the risk factor involved in facing the mighty upright beast while mining sent prices soaring as demand exploded. Adding more pressure, the Friends of the Gorillas are hollering "Ape" and threatening supplies, and in turn your most coveted gadget by far.

It has been 50 years since the original Xerox mass printing machine revolutionized the world. Technology today is bypassing our ability to increase productivity, as it requires functioning at higher speeds than our programmed capacity. Today's new machines can do miracles and almost print "organs on demand". Non-invasive ultrasound techniques can shake the brain into sending ions to troubled locations, and rewire the body by redirecting the nerves to take care of new reconstructions. Lucky for us baby-boomer generation, rock music may have guided our brain workouts and we weren't left out, with sound shockwaves and infrared disco lights during the inhaling blackouts.

Transistors today are so cheap in price, to a point that 100,000 of them cost less than a grain of rice. The transistor count in a Laptop is around 37 billion, catching up with our own brain neurons at 100 billion. Fast Tech is leaving many adult decision makers behind and blind, and yet they are expected to guide us and solve the economy as problems compound. How to manage the implications of technology on our future trends, and how do we solve what's moving faster than our ability to comprehend?

Regardless of ups and downs, 2011 is bound to bring happiness and charm, with the wedding in Westminster Abbey of Catherine and Prince William Charles. The famed London Cathedral served British Royalty since the great empire, and the show is bound to be world class with all the anticipated designer attires. Chile and its people gave us the ultimate uplifting, never abandoning hope and stamina of doing whatever it takes to bring the trapped miners through the ingenious capsule alive, as millions worldwide watched the miracle unfold live.

In sports earlier this year, the Mundial brought great soccer fame to Spain, par excellence winner of the tournament, as they gave spectators and fans worldwide great excitement. The Winter Olympics brought magic, fame and acclaim, as athletes broke records thought beyond attain.

In Texas the governor's race took on a different flavor, one entrepreneur candidate riding the hair waves to the campaign airwaves. In the end Governor Perry was re-elected to a new term as Texans appreciated his leadership and style, an impressive career come 2012 for a presidential bid with substance and style. A new mayor is at the helm in Houston, Lady Annise Parker packing a solid service background and selfless style, and winning the office with the help of the free wave lifestyle.

Our travels included Syria this year where the original alphabet was found, and where some of the most preserved roman forums and crusader forts are spread all around. Along the way a quick stop in Dubai to see the world's tallest tower from the ground. We had a chance to experience New York City again with a visit to MOMA, the museum a masterpiece of architecture, and a Mecca of modern art all through the galleries and halls. The rendition of Norma Jean is still on the large center wall, a fine tribute to the iconic Marilyn Monroe by Andy Warhol. Though New York is a successful high-rise city, the future to save energy may reside somewhere deep beneath the street grids of Midwest cities. Known as SubTropolis, the world's largest underground business complex is 100 feet below Kansas City, a fifty five million square feet metropolis of factories and offices operating on very little energy.

Revisiting our Moon, earth may still be bitter about a cataclysmic event of many moons past, when the Moon came into existence, as earth was forced to give up a chunk of its own substance. The origins of the Moon have been in debate for hundreds of years, and only recently have scientists accepted the conclusion of one of their peers: a large meteorite struck the earth and blew out parts of the sphere, rock scattered and matter got pulverized, but the debris recollected itself and re-synthesized, forming the 2,000 miles wide planet forever romanticized.

The same may have happened to planet Venus at some point in its past, so massive the meteorite collision that it literally reversed the "spin" of Venus to the opposite direction in one hellish blast. Though earth may have given the moon a bit of its round, around 500 BC and with only insight, Aristotle figured out the earth must be round since no other shape can cast the crescent shade on the Moon circling around.

Looking ahead we'll need to do some galactic travels, especially with our planet at risk of interstellar collision a few millenniums ahead. Last year the Crystal looked to the inner earth Magma as a propeller to send earth out of orbit and safer grounds. It is quite conceivable the Magma will change its East-West rotation into North and South, sending our North Pole to the Equator, an instant polar ice meltdown on a grand global showdown. Getting to outer space is no easy feat, though it has been on scientists minds seriously for well over fifty years. At the

Orion Project of that time, they surmised that to get to far away planets, space shuttles need the propulsion of atomic power as a series of explosions of nuclear bombs, in timed sequences to propel the space ship at such high speeds to get us to the next planet in a couple of months. Unfortunately and to halt space nuclear explosions, President Kennedy signed the treaty with Russia on non-nuclear proliferation, and the dream is stuck till some future generation.

Experiments for high speeds through CERN are quite near, as the European Organization for Nuclear Research is ready to test the Hadron collider in Switzerland sometime next year. Protons at high speed will circle the collider to recreate some of what we see in space, and maybe we can move beyond the biblical and finally see the original formation of a universe out of shear space. As with any science on the edge, look out for the possibility that the collider may create black holes and suck our earth inwards to somewhere else with no boundaries or walls.

As global warming remains in our hot pursuit, today's scientists are busy trying to figure how we can get to a moving asteroid and hitch a ride, to save the fuel until we cross the galactic divide. The Crystal Ball is banking on an easier trick to get us out of the near term warming trend, by nudging earth into a wider rotation orbit around the sun, distant enough to compensate for the increasing intensity of its cosmic guns.

The next threat to us may come from the internet, the web keeps getting more tangled up that at some point it may implode on itself, and becomes a black hole for our stored knowledge and saves. Where will all our records go, will they get lost in the dark or disappear as thin air quarks? If all you have is there, you live in cyberspace, and you need a cyber executor for your estate.

Social media is working so fast that stories disappear as the next buzz appears, and it can jam the internet in emergencies. We have become virtual people known by our cell phones and credit cards, and they form our national ID cards. Nowadays it seems only the now and the future are at the fore, and we are in an age where there is no time for history anymore. Societies worldwide are raising the standards of living and marching in step as one block, the electronic gismos maintaining one speed for the civilization clock.

Timelessness may be our quest next year. Woodstock will be forty years in 2011, and two of our perennial rock superstars are senior citizens, Mick Jagger is sixty seven and Keith Richard sixty six. They can still catapult the Rolling Stones to top the charts. The best Prime Time was run by a seventy seven year old with pant straps a signature to which he still clings, Larry King. The Male Bra, otherwise known as the Jockstrap, was patented in 1897 and yet millions are sold every year still, some as fun birthday gifts to friends on the magic pill.

Life never ceases to give us chances to make mistakes and learn from them. Our compassion is continually taxed to the limit with all the demands of how to perfect this planet and reduce poverty, and move millions to better destiny. At times we could be our worst enemy, yet our legacy is our work and the people associated with us and who make us happy, and to all of you who share the ride and embrace friendship, I wish you a happy season and a fabulous holiday as we sail together on the stellar 2011 ship.

Imad F. Abdullah, AIA, December 2010

The Year 2009

2009 CAME UPON US WITH much anticipation and expectation. It has been a year of spectacles: the spectacular presidential inauguration, the spectacle of a world all shook up over the precarious economic balance with equities hanging like stalactites awaiting their meltdown, and the once formidable stock market down last March to test the double bottom earlier drop, uncertain how far down to stop. The Flu pandemic with its spread out tentacles proved too hard to tackle, the late arriving vaccine distributed at random too slow to halt the pandemonium. Escalating wars are an open wound refusing to heal, and to top it all piracy off Somalia's high seas.

Afghanistan continues to be a hotbed for zealots in bed with politicians and tribal heads, winning or losing still far ahead, and controlling the future of death is still an elusive bet. Trying to manage a conflict and internal strife from a safe zone, pilots from California are guiding the drones.

Iran remains on the radar screen a big spectacle, their positions deemed rigid and intractable. The intricacies of the nuclear political game are head to head with the rug makers of old fame, already seasoned in the art of weaving hundreds of knots per square inch and adept at the art of fusing colors in intricate patterns with every thread. At times a weaving clan, sometimes accused of running a happy poppy plant, craftsmen of Qom with their spare time went about stitching Plutonium.

Exporting democracy is a tough sell as it can become a great divide. Handed down to an Iraq in transition and worn out after seven years of war and internal strife, Iraq is experiencing the trials and tribulations of an imperfect Democracy. Fair representation is a tough icon to achieve in a multicultural theocracy. North Korea is in a fading mode, the newscasts toning down the nuclear conflict in hopes of lowering the confrontation level and moving negotiations forward. Can there be a future to adversaries, or will high-tech become the Equalizer? History is in the making, and we'll see who writes the last chapter of North Korea, whether the sensible folks of Wikipedia or some pundit from the wicked media.

China celebrated the sixtieth anniversary of The Revolution: the body of Chairman Mao preserved for would be eternity remains on display in the glass cage awaiting the next round when he could return to power. Rumor has it that it is a double of wax, an uncomfortable thought for his followers waiting for him to rise. The Chinese Zodiac pegs 2010 as the year of the tiger, a fearsome animal of the woods and a symbol of strength and vicious moods. On this side of the ocean, a golfing Tiger went into hiding deep in the woods, awaiting the calm after the storm from his multiple tigress wounds.

Turkey is on a quest for its rightful place as a regional power, shuffling several decks in hope of lining the aces. The Middle East is marking more time, it's been a year of search for the newest peace with Israel's new Prime Minister Netanyahu, as everyone is building networks and gambling on who's going to be the next who's who. One place where politics and religion mix well is Lebanon, so well the country can operate without a government for months at a time. Lebanon finally formed a new government, ministers and members of Parliament dividing religions into sects with equalized shares, allocating everyone a slice of the government timeshare.

Politics took a back seat to economics in a world of uncertain forecasts and fragile and unforgiving systems with record deficits and in search of handouts. Though scary most of the time, deficits do not necessarily cause inflationary pressure: Japan at one time had the highest debt ratio to Gross Development Product and still had zero inflation, Italy and Belgium had higher deficits than US but lower inflation. France is a special case: its' debt to GDP is nearly equal to the US but with half the inflation rate. Their precious Bordeaux and exclusive Chateaux wines work their magic on the mind, substituting the splurge at the malls to unwind with the pleasures of the fancy gruyere cheese and wine. If you're there on a visit, the list of the fabled Paris restaurant, La Tour D'Argent, weighs nine kilograms for their 15,000 bottles of the finest spirits. Please come in two hours ahead of your reservation time to make the selection of your dream wine.

Brazil's currency has been fairly strong, up thirty six percent against the Dollar this year, now becoming a hedge that Brazil placed a two percent tax on foreign portfolio investments. Brasilia celebrates fifty years in 2010, now a capital of high paychecks and still with the exclusive city plan of the renowned architect Oscar Niemeyer and President Kubitschek.

On a sad note for France and Brazil, 228 passengers and crew were lost at sea when Air France Flight 447 crashed into the Ocean on a flight from Rio de Janeiro to Paris.

In Venezuela, Argentina and other parts of South America, the growing barter economy is a welcomed change, no worries about currency or Gold to exchange. Speaking of Gold, Bretton Woods was immortalized in 1944 when it made the US Dollar the reserve currency, with a US commitment to redeem dollars at thirty five dollars per gold ounce. Though the US abandoned gold in 1971, the dollar still accounts for two thirds of the world's reserve currency. Foreign governments and central banks hold 62.6% of US Treasury Securities held by foreigners, not including individuals, and it is in their interest to protect the value of the Dollar, making collapse an unlikely matter.

At today's prices of eleven hundred dollars an ounce, Mr. Knox would have been real proud of his Fort Knox. The amount of their disclosed gold is 147.3 million ounces and a golden opportunity knocks. As voodoo economics would have it, this Gold is held as an asset of the US at book value of $42.22 per ounce. Tonnage aficionados can figure 5,050 tons, in about 368,000 standard 400 troy ounce gold bars. In an age of three trillion in deficits, gold is waiting to wipe our national debt once an ounce reaches twenty thousand dollars.

While Congress is scrambling to fill the bottom-less gap, Senator Roth made a name for himself some time back by reducing the load off the Taxpayers back. In 2010 law changes take effect, removing income limit restrictions and allowing anyone to convert to a Roth IRA with unlimited amounts. Switching IRA savings to Roth are estimated by the 2012 elections to reach umpteen digit Billions, a boon for candidate Obama on his second White House magic carpet ride with the new slogan: Deficit Reduction Pride. With so much debt the US needs a strong Military, not only for national safety but also for economic safety. Fighting the enemy is at one spectrum's end, and intimidating friendly countries and lenders holding US Bonds and dollars against an earlier cash-out is at the other end. Maybe the military can prevent the economy from going to hell and lend a hand to fight credit card fraud and identity theft just as well.

With the new Obama Presidency came a major changeover in administrations. Republicans ceded the seat of power to rival Democrats respectfully, handing over the transfer on that ceremonious day with dignity and tact, while one limb of the party was in a big rush to plot an ultimate republican comeback, better known as Rush Limbaugh. When Presidents move on, their undercover problems move up center stage, and the newly elected president can own up to them thereafter or push them forward 4 years to the next term. If elected again, extend the promise one or two years after the end of the new term, or let history be the judge and jury, and work diligently to build a favorable legacy.

Before the end of his first year, President Obama was awarded The Nobel Peace Prize, many wondering why and questioning the venerable Oslo establishment decision and how wise. In his short 9 months stretch, claims are President Obama diffused the tension with Russia over the planned anti-nukes in Eastern Europe, opened a dialogue with Iran and North Korea, changed the discourse with Cuba and made overtures to the Islamic world. Perspective wise and fair or not, it earned him a good shot at the prize. Another Nobel Laureate, President Carter is on a high, lately center stage as his ten percent unemployment record is being challenged but feeling vindicated as he did it with no wars or large deficits. He still holds the record for the prime rate at 21.5%. High unemployment generates many spectators who otherwise would be active Wall Street speculators, and dissent and criticism increase exponentially as every Dick and Harry and Alec act smart, with every new blip on the joblessness misery chart.

The spectacular markets comeback from the March lows was nothing short of miraculous considering that General Motors and Chrysler filed for bankruptcy, up eighty percent. Schoolteachers and others with large retirement funds recaptured much of the lost wealth, and the potential for an increase in theft and crime was contained under the bailout plan. Meanwhile, a speculator par excellence gave us the spectacle of a lifetime, with fifty billion disappearing live on the world stage in front of our eyes. Bernie Madoff pulled it off with a Houdini style bluff, and though he went to jail, investors are hanging onto the hope for the billions by the coattail. Another figure with only a seven billion figure in the "now you see it now you don't" money limelight, Allen Sanders may be next to jail and is on hold without bail.

Every October we celebrate a Monday with a splash, its twenty two year anniversary this time as the pundits like to remind us of how long it has been since that fateful Black Monday crash of October 1987". Investors this October reacted to positive earnings in the US and set a bullish tone across the globe. A giant flea market in its own right, Ebay is a children paradise, as many housewives sell kids toys and clothes while buying toys and clothes one size up, as the child goes through about three sizes a year growing up.

The spectacular rise and fall of a barrel of Oil $150 to $80 was a flaring spectacle. With the oversupply from refining, many wells are being drilled but completions postponed until prices firm up, postponing cost until it makes economic sense. Not yet ready to be an international oil company producing and selling, China is hoarding, buying reserves for the future as this diversifies them into crude oil and out of dollars. A jewel in the Middle East has less sparkle for now: after so much guts and audacity in building, Dubai defaulted on 60 Billion sending real

estate prices spinning and tumbling, and the eleva-
tors of the world's highest building were unable to
do the heavy lifting. In an earlier time and at the
southwestern end of the Saudi peninsula, the earliest
high rises appeared in Yemen, still witnessed in the
incredible World Heritage city of Shibam, a reminder
that Dubai may yet earn a spot as a future heritage
from 2009.

Global warming is facing a credibility test: was
climate change a function of climate changers hiding
and destroying adverse data? In retrospect, Warming
is bad for natural gas prices as speculators want cool
weather to create demand, and also bad for our health
as warmer weather is friendlier to the Flu virus. Bad
as it is, it is not the worst pandemic in recorded
history: the Spanish Flu of 1918-19 killed one third
of the world population, between forty million and
one hundred million died, more than WWI and II
combined. WWI may have ended because of it since
so many soldiers were sick or dying.

How much of the Greenland ice sheet and the
West Antarctic ice sheet might melt due to rising
temperatures? As Scientists explain, already the sea
level change is not uniform and varies from place to
place. Colder, denser and saltier, the North Atlantic
seawater is normally two feet lower than the northern
Pacific, maybe cleaner too. About one thousand miles
northeast of Hawaii a garbage patch roughly twice
the size of Texas is trapped in the swirling Pacific
current, and is doubling in size every decade forming
a giant whirlpool. So far five large such patches are
swirling around the oceans of the world. Maybe it's

the solution to our shortage of land dumps, permanent whirlwinds of manmade islands of our civilization refuse, a sobering display for future tourists on a cruise. No ifs or buts about it, and though they contribute little to global warming, cigarette butts make their own brand of pollution. Taking years to disintegrate, they spread pollutants and soot throughout the microcosmic world and pollute water and streams: worldwide 5.5 trillion cigarettes are puffed each year.

Though we worry about the shrinking "Green", concern should be from the stuff we don't see, the underground deep down, deeper still, going near damn the center of the earth: the molten uranium that is in the core of the planet. Much of the heat of the magna comes from what may be the super giant nuclear reactor there. The molten iron that flows between the core and the surface of the planet gives us picturesque Hawaii and other exotic volcanoes and is believed to cause the magnetic fields.

We could be in the early stages of a reversal of magnetic force lines that encircle earth. Their strength is already down ten to fifteen percent, a movement that appears to have intensified about one hundred and fifty years ago. The switch in the magnetic field is believed to be related to subterranean currents of the molten iron beneath. As scientists surmise, it may someday suddenly compress the inner core, which might increase the density of the unrefined uranium. The core could then reach the critical mass for a gigantic nuclear explosion, the spectacular spectacle of all spectacles.

During the reversal, the field slowly disintegrates

and then reappears with opposite polarity. North becomes South on the compass, and Heaven and Hell could trade places. The impact becomes unfathomable, especially the signals affecting birds, fish and migratory animals where the magnetic field is their Nav-Star. It happened before at least once in our very distant past but as it takes a few thousand years of transition, we're more likely to fire up and call upon evolution to help us survive it as a species.

Assuming we'll outlive the wobbly magnetism, astronomers predict that over the next hundred millions years, the sun will become increasingly hotter, and everything on earth may boil to become non-matter. As in the Green debate, scientific models are spread over a wide spectrum of time, within a billion years to 2.3 billion as the time experts would have us believe the precision of their research excerpts.

Science continues to rock, new products, discoveries and amazing achievements. Science stats tell us that the MRI scan is different for people who live in Florida versus Washington. Whereas Science wants to explain everything, the debate between science and religion continues, and when science and religion collide, it becomes the stuff of miracles. Science has even developed an explanation for miracles, as discoveries show that the plants which produced LSD were mixed at times with grains that people ate, creating hallucinations and the "believe it or not" miracle tales.

Science and religion are always uneasy colleagues: while science and research advance funeral by funeral, religion expands and spreads its heavenly world "funeral by funeral".

Since we still have plenty time before the ultimate demise let's look at our mundane issues of the day, especially as we just finished the wonderful Thanksgiving Turkey holiday. Gurus of the Turkey Genome Sequencing tell us that 9/10th of the genome have been mapped, while the chicken and cows and pigs have already been mapped. Our quest to comprehend the species remains in its infancy as our expert "Organismologists" tell us that ninety nine percent of creatures and sea organisms are unknown still.

For those concerned about a world without oil in one hundred years or so, the choke is in a whole different sphere and how electricity is produced: the magnets. The real short supply will come from a hence nebulous material: Neodymium, a component of strong permanent magnets, which are made out of a mixture of Neodymium, Iron and Boron. Fortunately for us humans, and as an electric engine of circuits and chemical substances, our brain puts out our own personal magnetic attraction, which keeps the world retail hopping as accessories and clothing styles are the hooks leading us to weddings and various other relationship settings.

Weddings are always a great time: happiness abounds, families expand, and new life gets a chance. Marriage continues to be the subject of studies and research, the married want to find out why it hasn't worked for others, singles wants to know why it worked for others, and the ravages of divorce or perennial bachelorhood ultimately controlling the fate of every one separating from their other.

Love and Marriage are no longer joined at the hip, as marriage is now the stuff of stats. The eager mongers developed a "marriage Index", a new bellwether replacing the bygone honeymooners Belle Weather. It is made up of a composite score to gage the health of marriage, 76.2 in 1970 versus 60.3 in 2008. Index components are heavily analyzed, but Love itself remains outside the bounds of the stats as the digital numbers are incapable of gauging starry eyes in a statistically significant manner.

Icons are hard to come by, and the higher they reach, the tougher when they depart on all of us as we shared with them some of our most memorable moments. This year has been one of fallen icons: Pop is mourning the king of pop Michael Jackson, we bid farewell to the ultimate Venus for a whole generation Farrah Fawcett Majors, and we'll miss the great orator of his time, Senator Ted Kennedy. They entertained us, enchanted us, and some overcame tragedies and great odds. They were with us in the right time of history when the flower children were blooming in the sixties, the Monterey Festival, Woodstock, and the surreal movie that stamped the generation, "Hair".

Their departure evokes memories of past icons, James Dean, Norma Jean who's best known as Marilyn Monroe, Jimmie Hendrix, Janis Joplin, Elvis Presley, Queen's lead Freddie Mercury, the incredible Jim Morrison of The Doors, and the renowned international Diva, Dalida. We lost them in their prime, and wonder how the world would have changed had they continued to be with us, and what direction would they have taken us. As they opened up the doors of history to claim their presence, history will keep their memory cherished for all of us to reflect upon, and to admire their talent, achievements, and personal courage. Today's music seems still in mourning, though bright spots shine the light periodically on the future.

Our own travels took us to a new destination this year: Lisbon mixes the glory of past heroism with the realities of a world with less imperialism. Its' Modern Architecture of the last fifty years is showing date and wear, a reminder that what we design for today's age may not live up to the demands of future societies tech stage. On a quick stop in Milwaukee we were entertained by enchanting friends, and a visit to the Harley Davidson Museum there was a reminder of earlier times, when the macho and pride was the thrill of a motorcycle ride.

Around the US, Healthcare is in Congress being dissected, politicians attempting to diagnose what's ailing medical care. Meanwhile insurance and the insured are confused and unsure, as their plans are customized to a new Congressional High Couture. With two thousand pages plus, the media is touting the healthcare bill as "politics by the pound". The bickering of Republicans and Democrats slows legislation and the Crystal Ball figures it is highly driven by worrying about future votes when the sector dependent on government programs grows.

A book does not a presidential candidate make.

Sara Palin is making the rounds lately, whether for future Senatorial ambitions, maybe a second vice or presidential spot, or the prelude to a second book to be written if there is a second Obama Administration. The ratings will guide, too early to speculate on this hound, especially with the Secretary of State Hillary looming in the background. In Texas the Governor's race is heating up, a hot subject for the Crystal of next year. Illegal immigration is bound to be in the debates, and as the high fence wall along Mexico's border makes it too hard and costly for illegals in the US to cross back over, they forgo vacations and stay permanently on the US side of the border.

Earth took a breather this year contemplating its mean actions of the last two years. Hurricane Ike's impact remains deeply felt, and as the seventeen foot waves of the time destroyed so many roofs, our Flood Insurance went through the roof. In Houston, our highly contested Mayoral Run-off election was finally settled with no dispute, the two candidates in the run-off straddling the spectrum from the gay life-style pursuit to the pin striped suit. Lady Parker won the day, and her reputation could increase incoming gay migration and put pressure on real estate. "Sex and Real Estate" may be a new discipline in the making.

By some estimate, and based on DNA studies and a little assumption, one out of every 218 of us is a descendent of one person, a great warrior with the most formidable empire in history, Genghis Khan. We may be all a large pool of distant cousins and relatives, and our vast world is too connected to be split into bits and bytes as the sum of the parts is one earth, our final frontier. As it may expire in a billion years, it is the ultimate ship to be steered to safe cosmic orbit. Maybe we'll activate the mean magnetic molten lava to explode through one pole, sending rocket earth out of the trap of the sun's orbit and into some other galaxy or through a black hole, where we can safely coast for few more billions, enjoying the spending of our newly minted bail-out trillions.

Life is for us to live while we scramble to maintain systems and learn manuals of this electronic survival age, and how to carry the brain software indefinitely when we can't easily update the body hardware. The wise one once said: good judgment comes from experience, and experience comes from bad judgment. Keep experimenting, stay on the good side, call your shots with wisdom and take your lumps in stride, it's all a part of the journey and this once in a lifetime ride. May luck remain on your side, and I wish you happy holidays and a prosperous new year with nothing but upside.

Imad F. Abdullah, AIA December 2009

The Year 2008

2008 HAS BEEN A PERPLEXED year, with Olympic Games, elections and hurricanes, and grand melt-downs. Casino life and the Las Vegas fame were no match for the wonder and excitement of the New York startling money game.

Starting with what's on everyone's mind, many are squeezed out financially in a tight wedge, teetering anxiously as Wall Street fell off the edge. Where did all the money go and is it only a paper loss? Was it all before a paper gain, or was there a greenback to be had between the multifold layers of derivatives and swaps, or are we in a big swamp? How to recapture some of luster lost in the panic and prevent another nasty downward trounce?

Wall Street showed up in Olympic form, records shattered in split-second time, stocks behaving like spent athletes cascading on chart lines all the way to ever lows with no "finish line". Cut to single digit size, the Big Three US auto makers are on the brink, battered and bruised and pleading for a handout, Unions on one side strapped on the bumpy ride and

bankruptcy is looming across the divide, the precipice too steep and not much leeway left to budge.
With retirement plans reduced to sledge, blue chips
lost their edge, as they tumbled with such a magnitude that even Hedge funds couldn't hedge. How to
pull up the nest egg back to the highs of the chart
line, get to the retirement deadline and enjoy the
worry free pastime?

Interest rates have been on sale all year, few takers
with the economy in low gear. No more clogging
along as a rinky-dink lightweight, the national debt
is rejoicing well for now it has become a real heavy-
weight, the "billion here and a billion there" now
moved up to "a trillion here and a trillion there",
pretty soon almost real money. Trillions are now
household words, Uncle Sam treating his siblings
with such largesse that everyone is claiming to be a
close and deserving relative.

"Guaranteed by the Full Faith and Credit of the
United States Government" was at stake: Uncle Sam
rolled over Wall Street to shore up its namesake and
reassure bond holders and far away World States.
Whether Republicans or Democrats, they cannot
mess with either credit or faith: at a cost of only thirty
billion in annual interest, they voted seven hundred
billion dollars in handouts, one heck of a congressional leveraged buyout. Hold on to your bonds, no
reason to rush to cash and get out of town, there is
nowhere to hide if it's a world financial meltdown.

With so many trillions afloat the Dollar is heading
south, but hard assets and stocks are bound to compensate. Though real estate foreclosures are bounti-

ful so far, flagship fire sales are hard to come by, and good selections ought to be grabbed right now. Gold has not yet soared, inflation fears still not high on the mind when there is no money to fuel the demand. The Crystal Ball foresees the financial markets bottom to have already been at hand, though testing it again soon is not far- fetched as it is only a line in the sand. Nine months from now we could look back if we missed these opportune times, curse the market to go down at least one more time for us to load on stocks big time.

For the US as a whole, the cost of buying international influence is beginning to exceed the means. As the US economy searches for a crutch, the world is in turmoil and the clash of civilizations is expanding to encompass religion and capitalism. Can Democracy survive without the ability to print money, and will developing countries importing it go belly-up chasing their opportunity?

Never known to be gentle or kind, nor predictable or benevolent in rough times, oil gave us the ride of a lifetime. Hopes for nuclear energy and wind power are diminishing as alternative energies, and "Green" is puzzled where to go from here to get more synergy. As the earth a few mills back changed course from the circular rotation around the Sun to the twenty five thousand years elliptical mode cycle, polar ice was bound to increase as it did for millenniums of years, but CO_2 warming the atmosphere was counterbalancing the mean ice age ellipse. Recession has become CO_2's enemy as gas demand dropped and fewer fumes pollute the air, but in retrospect, it allows more years for fossil fuels to crank the engines between the sporadic bouts of fresh air.

Enough on the money talk, and moving sideways to the twenty four hour talkative shows, presidential debates gave us good entertainment and slapstick, America riding high on the newest imaging and sarcasm: Lipstick. Governor Palin stole the show while she lasted, blowing like a hurricane on the plain campaign of the battered republican McCain. President elect Obama's campaign appears to have been sustaining the economy quite well, and once his victory loomed clear and the ratings bode him well, markets collapsed and bid their depositors farewell.

President Obama qualified himself for the job through organizational skills and winning debates, proving that the president in the US is not the smartest or the most educated, but the most electable among willing candidates. As he surrounds himself with brains to carry his policy, he is keeping the competition close to the heart to watch it closely. After pulling former President Clinton heavyweights, it is time to screen future White House interns, after one then famous sideshow turned fatal and almost ended Clinton's show.

Hillary got the Secretary of State prize, uncertain whether it's a happy end or a new beginning for future presidential drives. As if to show its resentment, Wall Street dropped nearly 700 points on the day of the announcement. With so many claiming to be agents of change who tipped Obama's scale, The Crystal ball expects a future clash among the multitude of constituencies over entitlement and the spoils of power, a serious scenario to counter come the next election hour.

The legacy of President Bush straddles the pundits acclaim, the remaining time too short to retrieve the tribulations of his two terms reign. Too much to undo, too little time, but maybe the presidential library will ease up the judgment of history, given enough time. Unfortunately for President Bush, there was so much term left at the end of the money, and he could no longer count on prosperity to buy out a legacy.

As the sun sets temporarily on her career, and as she sails into a yet uncharted horizon, Secretary of State Condi is riding into the sunset seemingly still no clear direction of policy As politicians patiently serve their terms and eagerly await a generous book deal, doubtless an offer is on her table to sign and seal. Doing it the easy way, Governor Palin went through a short and sassy cycle, cut through the mustard and got a sweetheart of a deal for her upcoming block-buster title.

Many TV and talk radio programs and the like continuously piped political entertainment to the masses through television, the media becoming the perfect channel to provide tunnel vision. Media Control went to the extreme with national coordination in the last few weeks and days, as sensitive issues disappeared from the debates.

Soap opera took a political meaning as an extended series throughout the primaries and elections. Now thereafter, TV is busy analyzing "how it analyzed" these events and the conventions. Back in the limelight every now and then, perennial Barbara Walters can steal the show whenever and when. Her "Ten Most" comes now at the end of the year when everything is crystal clear and only the spin remains, a bit too late and somewhat in arrears. Much has been said about Bill Ayers, the University of Illinois at Chicago professor of questionable fame, nothing yet said about how a board of regents granted the appointment to such a resume behind his name.

As the seat of so much ecclesiastical clout, the Vatican was headlines as the Pope sought the faithful in America and spread his goodwill to all, a sight to behold especially for Catholics as faith in the divine sets their soul free in the presence of the Holy See.

On the world stage, France's President Sarcozy is having the time of his life, roaming the world with his new model wife. Cuba's Fidel is passing the torch, while Venezuela's Chavez wants more tenure to preach from the presidential porch. India and Pakistan are locked into a balance of power enforced by the existence of nuclear power, an uneasy pact as governments have to contend with pressure from foreign powers. They are practically tied at the hip, not many ways to escape the Mumbai zealots on their hellish trip.

China took the Olympics to different heights, adding several notches and raising the bar on the future host city as games in the Bird's Nest were elevated way far by athlete stars. The challenge is crystal clear as future competition is in economic might and who gets to feast, as performance requires countries to think Olympian to go head-to-head with the Far-East. In China and Russia, former bastions of communism, fortunes are experiencing the gyrations of Capitalism. From the highs above or maybe the deeps below, Stalin and Lenin are pounding: see I told you so.

Iraq is almost a haunted house, trials and debates a daily grind, and the '09 surge a reminder of the surge in Vietnam, by then President Nixon to force negotiations on Hanoi's strong man. Qatar may be the answer to the much touted exit strategy, where the military can reside and have long term cheap energy. Iran is on the sidelines, wondering when it will become headlines once again. For their nuclear everyone is up in arms, a good reason to showcase a threat and build more arms.

Lebanon has a new president, the Military once again the backbone of that democracy, supplying the "General" to head the uneasy truce between dissimilar groups. The clock will be anxiously ticking in 09 in the land of the Cedar, too much on the plate to have a peace without absolute support of the new leader. Next door, a sinister tool was used to oust the former Prime Minister, "Skeletons in the closet" a good weapon to effect a change of policy, as Israel is on another try with Prime Minister Livni.

The war on poverty has always been a misnomer, as only prosperity stops discontent and embraces factions, and channels frustration to productive action. Otherwise, political might is the only ticket to financial health, and everyone needs a political party to grab at the wealth. "Worldwide" needs more middle class to salvage peace in lieu of conflict and confrontation, and to stop unproductive condemnations.

Last year The Crystal Ball attempted to place a perspective on our universe, where some scientists estimated that there might be 125 billion galaxies. As light travels six trillion of our land miles a year, the universe was pegged at approximately fourteen billion light years across, and at 84,000,000,000,000,000,000,000 miles, it is a wide spread give or take a few strides.

Backtracking on the time line, we can't seem to be too sure about the exact time of the famed Big Bang, possibly in the vicinity of ten to fifteen billion years ago. In creating matter, scientists have temperature all figured out: about the first 10 to the -43 fraction of that Big Bang second (10 followed by 43 zeroes), the temperature was 100 million trillion degrees Fahrenheit, and Gravity was born. In the next few fractions of that same second, and as temperature was dropping to one billion billionth degree, matter emerges in the form of electrons and quarks and the electromagnetic force appears. By the time we're down to the one Trillion degrees, protons and photons formed, and a minute later, at one billion degrees, Helium, Lithium and Hydrogen.

Following our ancestors through time, earth assembled itself around 5 billion years ago, bio-life around 3.4 billion years, and about 700 million years multi-cellular plants and animals came about. Our humanoid ancestor appeared 15 million years hence, and we've finally arrived to Homo sapiens only 100,000 years from whence. A century and a half ago life expectancy was 37 years, as evolution was not concerned with our longevity, but only in reproduction to maintain our species, as grandparents past thirty seven years of age would then compete with their siblings for food supplies. Our physical make up was not of concern to evolution and perfection thereafter evaded us, let alone having a biological warranty. An economic recession may be good for our health: recession creates stress, which may force evolution to continue our mutative advancement to a better physical specimen.

Visionaries tell us that the rate of technical progress is doubling every decade, and the rate of change is accelerating. At today's rate, the one hundred years of progress of the twentieth century would equal twenty years, and the next twenty years will be achieved in only fourteen years, then in seven. At this rate of exponential growth, the twenty first century could move us forward 20,000 years of progress, a phenomenal reason to stick around.

Space is not the only domain of zeroes upon zeroes. The journey this year takes us into seldom-charted territory where, in the world of nanotechnology, space and time are being narrowed to infinitesimal limits, giving hope that we may finally invade the inner workings of our systems for the ultimate frontiers. Technology at the leading edge is exploring what it takes to start reverse engineering the brain, possibly uploading the mind onto some advanced future techno machine.

Which leads us to our human brain after three billion years of evolution: we're told it combines digital and analog methods of computations done through 100 trillion inter-neural connections. Conceivably, each can be processing information simultaneously. Granule cells in the cerebellum, the smallest neurons are packed about 6 million per square millimeter, and a single cubic millimeter of cerebral cortex may contain on the order of five billion synapses of different shapes and sizes. In 2020, we could be sending billions of nanobots into the brain to collect the info and maybe start the upload. Time is on our side, at least for those who will be around to witness the miracles of time.

Our family travels took us to Barcelona and Seoul this year, enchanting places though operating on totally different gears, the old world charm and easy style in contrast to a new world with a fast lane lifestyle. Back home and on Saturday September 13, Houston landed in the eye of the tiger, hurricane Ike laser focused on the Texas coast from several days out, the eye passing barely to the east of town. Awaiting doomsday is an eerie feeling, believing the weather experts hard to do when the predictions are off the charts. Right they were, and going through it was a survival experience for many. We're still in the aftermath, many silently carrying the load of rebuilding shattered lives.

Natural disasters are part of life, and at such times we relate well to the families and relatives of those who perished when Cyclone Nargis in Myanmar killed 130,000 and the Wenchuan earthquake in China nearly 70,000. Unfair and unjust, it's an eternal question of why and when, and why then.

As we continue our quest for self-actualization and getting ourselves up to par, the big challenge is how to understand and maximize what we are. Meanwhile and in line with the US government pledge for better times ahead, please accept a trillion New Year wishes as a bail-out prosperity package instead. Forward and onto the good times with a simple coin flipside, use it as a token down payment for the future upside.

One last time back to Wall Street, and maybe some astute cheers for an event of some one hundred years: History buffs may recall one famed financier, Henry Clews and his book in 1908 "Fifty Years on Wall Street", where he investigated the American stock panics of 1812, 1823, 1825, 1837, and 1857. Recapping the financial credit crisis of 1907 and the panic which ensued: "too much credit for the redeemable cash and too much speculation and reckless expansion". Many railways and industrial companies were forced to liquidate their holdings, and insolvent firms and institutions were wound up.

The cure he argued: "More Lending".

Happy New Year.

Imad F. Abdullah, AIA December 2008

The Year 2007

HAVING SO MUCH "WORLD" around us makes it challenging to go around every time. In search of clues, the Crystal Ball is going beyond to some distant past, and will interpolate from some of the recent science stats. Though so much on earth has happened, this may be best remembered as the year our universe secrets unraveled.

Looking into the sky, the Galaxies, and the expanse, the "wow factor" is found everywhere. Along the way, Zodiacs float in the stratosphere, filling incoming astro-wishes from the spinning sphere, everyone eager for wonderful and good news to hear. Though the Crystal Ball normally ponders the wonders for inspiration, year end is a good time to wonder about the wonder of it all, and the magnitude of the where and how.

Exploring our universe, the orbiting Hubble Space Telescope recently looked back in time at a tiny section of the southern sky, taking a visual core sample of the unknown, the edge of what is known. It looked twelve billion light years back, to a time one or two billion of our calendar years after the yet unfathomed Big Bang, and in that small segment of the sky it spotted 620 galaxies, by all counts one massive gang. Scientists full of excitement did what they do best, lining in queue to spread scientific clues to the clueless, and extrapolated from the sample that there might be 125 billion galaxies over the whole universe, floating in an expanding space. Looking up some can be seen, others can only be a dream, the distance in light years not simple even for logarithm.

The Crystal Ball will attempt to place a perspective on speed and space, an exercise in subliminal vision, as light travels six trillion miles a year in oblivion. Our Milky Way Galaxy, where we're all contained with our trials and tribulations, disputes and arguments, is less than 7,000 light-years thick, and about 80,000 to 120 000 light-years across, the extra-terrestrial gravity rallying its 30 million planets and stars in one giant Noah Ark.

For number crunchers and serious imagination, the universe at approximately 14 billion light years across is a stimulating visual of zeroes upon zeroes, 84,000,000,000,000,000,000,000 miles, more mind-boggling zeroes kilometer style, the unknown beyond a puzzle as a voyager to that frontier needs an eternal while.

2007 was also a year of powder kegs. Some are boiling to the rim, others still simmering, some standing still. The Globe is rotating around a not so simple political axis, one vertical trilateral Putin – Bush - Chavez axis with all 3 vying for both ends, and one horizontal axis Ahmadinejad and Bush at opposite ends. On the horizontal and the vertical of the cross, the quest for peace is a delicate balance to spread all across.

The Big Bear was awakened again, with much oil to spare, the return to global cooling a challenging and serious scare. Out of the ashes rose again the now friendlier KGB, with plenty money and honey for all the bees, smoothly watching the gate and its keys. In Venezuela, Chavez is on a perennial quest to stay permanent in the presidential nest, always seeking the limelight to convince voters he is best. South America's big brother Brazil is flexing economic might and ability, becoming a heavy hitter in world affairs with much prominence and stability. Argentina is prosperous again, the Paris of the South high on wine and Tango, the past currency blues and inflation a memory of a bygone era that seems now so long ago.

Iraq remains red hot with the factions on opposite tractions, recalcitrant positions preventing retractions. Many kegs are still boiling and fired up, brewing new start-ups. Fresh troupes were added to scoop the dissenting factions, no more love and attraction. In Parliament dissent is rampant, how to grant Multi-nationals a pass to explore and produce oil through the wreckage, and repair collateral damage.

Straddling Afghanistan and Pakistan, Binladen is a faint blip on the radar screen, finding him no longer policy mainstream. After fading from memory Afghanistan is back selling "get high" expensive bread, while Pakistan is testing the limits of international friendship as democracy snails ahead, under

the watchful eye of the newly elected, sitting government head. The end of that chapter is not seen
yet, although another chapter on North Korea is
closing well. Nuclear power is a sensitive issue, as it
has been the ticket for the 5 permanent seats on the
UN Security Council. No more desired in The Club,
North Korea was hungry to make the switch and
negotiate out, abdicating its nuke in favor of world
acceptance and a handout. The brawl of the Ahmadinejad showdown is cooling down with the recent
rhetoric slowdown, maybe Peace finally struck a deal
with Syria and Iran.

Happy times are in France again, as a newly
"bachelored" President is at the helm. The would-be
first lady made a tough choice, the presidential palace
no match for her divorce. The French may claim the
crown of the sensual but when it comes to hiring at
the revered Elysee palace, ask "Bill" for guidance and
advice on how can Sarcozy keep desire on ice.

After six years off, the Light to get the Middle
East peace re-processed is on again, the tunnel so far
is too long for light to reach the end. Peace has a new
home after the Camp David 1 and 2 trips, the scripts
updated for Annapolis with sequel clips. Lebanon
remains an intransigent powder keg experimenting
with a new form of governance, a country with no
head. Dividing Lebanon is on the table still where
some minorities may become majorities again, a dra-
conian and radical change if they can't stitch a unity
government for a happy end.

A Star is losing some of its stripes, as the
esteemed Secretary of State Condi appears to fluctu-

ate on issues, unable to get signatures on the dotted lines. The push in order to pull subjects to the sphere requires many treks, one more year left for Condi's legacy on how to successfully shuffle the decks.

With so many powder kegs, global warming is hot on the front row again. The polar ice mixed the signals with a late Freezing Spring Storm in the US, followed by a hot summer and more snow in the Northeast. Confused by now, earth needed to vent some CO_2; Santa Ana took the hint and blew the winds with evil will, fanning the flames on the exclusive Malibu hills. Fate, normally a democratic institution, is not playing everyone on a level field, but "California Dreaming" remains a powerful magnetic field.

On the look-out for a cheerful end, a former V.P. and presidential dark horse is quietly grazing accolades till the Democratic convention. The cool Al Gore basks in the glory of a Nobel, getting the original "Dynamite Award" over the controversial open ozone hole to the Black Holes upward. Alternative energy is gaining steam, much talk now that oil is near $100. If it can only push to $200, we'll live on wind and tidal wave energy, the Sun powering more synergy. Sunlight still has its advantages per modern science: when combined with increased vitamin D it may reduce the risk of "17 types of cancer". Between "win and lose", how to pick life, how to choose.

The universe of capitalism is under scrutiny. Along the specter, capitalism remains at risk in poorer countries, fine and flowing in industrialized countries, and at risk again in small super rich countries. The power of capital can create much action to smooth international interaction.

In the universe of stocks, where a billion dollars is a drop in the economy, the "Light Dollar" is the answer for more liquidity, as the value continues the slide to infinity, the Euro flying too high for sound parity. The streams of freshly minted dollar bonds are losing their stride, but the dollar remains a world currency so much traded worldwide, making the process easy for cash bribes. Europe is paying less for oil in Euros with the Dollar slide, a present from President Bush to the G-7 tribe. We're all paying for the war at the pump, the money chest is a trust practically, when countries at the receiving end repatriate dollars buying for their military, and saving for the future wonder drug, nuclear technology.

Hovering near a high most of the year, Wall Street beat its record this year. American infrastructure stocks sank low as the spans are not strong enough to bridge rivers and seas, and funds are invested in turbulent sinkholes overseas. Please call Congress to fill the jar, for Architects and Engineers to bring the bridges up to par.

The hype for the race to the White House is in full pageantry, leading the horses so far Lady Hillary. After many flacks in debates, riders realized they will not be desired as vice presidential candidates, Richardson still possibly the least controversial as a "back-up" mate. The scene is getting more ferocious, while the cool and collected Bill Clinton awaits his new role as "the President's date". Candidates appear in the dark on US policy matters and serious briefings, wallowing in the debates with uncertain leanings. Ratings remain in flex, the "he said she said" becoming entertainment at its best, sometimes a serious show, other times a candy show.

The pundits anchored by TV are out to weed the candidates, highlighting embarrassing moments of their history, a media privilege to affect world policy. The role of media as a watchful eye of the system evaporated under centralized partisan ownerships, the "yes or no" and "with or against" are the interview style in short blips.

For next year's serious debates, and as the candidate choices become quite clear, estate taxes will fill our ears, as they expire in a couple of years. Otherwise, Congress may have to pass legislation to put death on hold until a new law takes hold. The Crystal Ball envisions the two Wall Street darlings to be in the final race, Hillary and Giuliani as co-stars of pop rock, until one pops the Champagne cork, since they both serve the capital of stocks and corporate pork, New York.

Immigration has been two-edged, what to do before legalization, how to get the votes thereafter. A new phenomenon is at play, with legal immigration over the years producing voting blocs uncertain which way to sway. To even out voting power, a new politic is geared at different factions within the foreign country of origin, as seen in Armenia, Turkey, and the Kurds. Splitting the vote is key to keep the 2 party hegemony, a new art for effective foreign policy.

In sports, we witnessed the World Rugby Cup this year, passionate games held once every 4 years.

China's Olympics are gaining speed, 2008 now the focus of world athletes. A new hero in Olympic form is already there at the scene, no longer content with only 40 thieves. The famous Ali Baba has come alive in China, Alibaba.com becoming China's biggest commerce site, the stock offering nearly rivaling one famous IPO a few years back when Google.com was brought to light.

Speaking of Google, this new Galileo is charting the universe with angels of the skies, as Google Earth this year launched Google Sky. What to do with this Galileo Googa-lei when the web is his esquire, how to keep the tribes coming to the holy corral in search of the light, when Googlers surf the web all night.

For Houston, the agony of high oil elsewhere continues to fuel its economy everywhere. Non-stop flights to Moscow and Dubai were launched from here, Doha and other distant destinations in line for non-stops next year. As our Dynamo soccer team has won the national championship 2 years in a row, get ready for a new venue along our Stadiums Row. And Houston is once more eye-balling a re-tooled form of land re-organization, as higher density projects again test the limits of the inner "not in my back yard" gen-eration.

On our earth, how lucky we are not to exist at the speed of light, where we can still smell the roses day and night. The Sixties generation is now in their sixties, the trip has taken a full generation. While some then borrowed light for Speed, most became "Knights in White Satin", some have "flowers in their hair", and few single still, "Standing in the Shadow of Love", and rolling stones for a lucky strike to fall again in love.

Reflecting back on life and what's important, friendship and family are our personal gravity, anchoring and holding us as one band, in a world being pulled apart by remnants of manmade big bangs". Let's keep it together, enjoy the holiday and have a cheer, there will always be the challenge of a new year.

Imad F. Abdullah, December 2007

The Year 2006

2006 HAS BEEN THE YEAR the engines went in reverse. A year of contradictions and shifting gears and many tears, it was in one word, "unraveling".

In Iraq, where chemistry defies physics and logic, heaven took to the sky while hell reigned supreme. The situation is becoming extreme with different factions rallying around their sect and vying to control a mirage dream. The brutality of war, the sheer magnitude of death, and the stepchild civil wars are mesmerizing everyone. Wars are a silencer, emotions get too charged, and it's a shut down until the dust settles and the day of reckoning arrives: where, what, and who did when, pity the time.

The year challenged long held political theories of war and peace: the number of US soldiers upwards of 150,000 for Iraq not enough to quell, and doubtful that sending more will dispel the vengeful spell. It has become an American dilemma with not a bright spot, only attempts at controlled chaos. With few partners left to dance, the pre-war strategy guidance is running out of substance, and the marching dunes of desert sand are proving too much for the former lines drawn in the sand.

The limits of power always get tested in faraway lands in need of too much manpower. Where to drum up soldiers, as bad credit and high debt disqualify many from serving the nation, lest they be manipulated when vulnerable to pay-off temptation. As the length of service gets long and more fallen brought home, the war legacy is shrinking, magnified by the mass memorials of Iraqi unknowns. The ultimate soldier James Baker is back charting with great skill of mind a war passed to a new president, when history may be more kind.

It won't be long before future technology renders today's war machines obsolete. Future computer wizards are manipulating hitherto unknown viruses, shutting down codes and sparking complex nodes. How long before everyone wears chips as protection means, and maybe have personal laser beams? The window for war may be for ten years hence beyond which comes the unconventional, as the weapons of war become too multi-dimensional: holographic soldiers could be beamed to the battlefield, images unreal fighting with shadowy zeal and no blood to heal: the ultimate action war, surreal.

The first nuclear murder took place this year, science in pursuit and Interpol following suit. Moscow is off limits for now until the British figure it out, how the former Russian spy was knocked out and whether the order was from highest up: nuke-him-out. Everyone is concerned about the spread of the nuclear though it may be the next energy wonder. Australia is a ready client down-under with twenty five nuclear plants about 2020, give- or-take a number. The hype may only be to protect lucrative atomic technology sales, limit competition and grab bigger shares.

Always news are the nuclear top actors, Iran and North Korea on stage at the center of the reactor, with Russia and China a supporting cast, their UN veto power a balancing factor. Fallout from nuclear clouds is heavy on their minds come the US war with Iran. Reality is finally striking it's only a matter of when oil is back spiking, this time with no downtime as the "all out" is bound to be fearsome destiny fighting. Volatility abounds, and the coveted pipelines to be built behind safe soldiers lines are outside the turbulent frame of present times.

Bin-Laden remains on vacation, seemingly forgotten as the rapid-fire events overshadow his hibernation. For a while last year Iraq took a back seat only to capture us with the year-end execution of its captured president Saddam Hussein. Meanwhile a thirty three day war just happened between Israel and Lebanon. Out of nowhere as it was portrayed, a war ensued, improvised, and contrived. Lebanon remains a hot spot, a large unknown civilian tomb after much innocent blood was blasted by the blind cluster bombs. Democracy of the streets is pounding chapter upon chapter with masses living on the street. The home of "Democracy in Confusion" is unraveling, the tribes carrying the patriot religions to the nowhere unknown and faithfully marching.

As invading Lebanon was not a cakewalk, Israel is

shifting gears and brainstorming the think tanks, the military uncertain what to do with their vulnerable war tanks. Blaming Israeli Prime Minister Ohlmert went nowhere for he's no General, and the debacle was craftily overshadowed with events fired up in lands overwhelmed and in the gallows. Everyone in the troubled Holy Land remains on edge seemingly at war every day, when blood is the fuel for escalating into high gear and factions are on standby with full military gear. General Sharon now lingers in bed following a stroke that took him out of commission, history now the jury and the judge on his legacy following his Lebanon's failed mission.

India's new prosperity demands cooler heads and slow hand military threats, as protecting prosperity is more important than fighting to annex more poverty. Reversing long held one-way gears, Kashmir is on the table now with Pakistan, both sides in a better frame of mind. China's former cold shoulder is on the burner as cross visits along this multibillion human axis intensify, friendlier politics a welcome change from talking wells run dry. Darfur and Sudan remain tied in a war of the clans, the gears unable to deliver, a plague of sorts ravaging the survivors of past hunger plagues. Counting the dead is a daily whisper to a world so desensitized and unable to stem the flood of so much blood. The New World Order is featuring prosperous and hungry countries side by side, a formula for future suicide.

Illegal immigration between the US and Mexico, a misnomer for "willful trespass", continues to swim rivers and climb each mountain pass. Sewer and drainage lines connecting border cities are sometimes underground human pipelines, some large enough for vehicles to go by. What to do above ground, when the underground evades the battleground? Maybe it's time to set up agencies such as admit-a-staff along Border States where legal work permits can fill the supply with dignity and grace, in lieu of hunger and disgrace.

In Cuba and as Fidel may pass, for now having to pass to brother Raoul as new head of the aging revolutionary class. Optimism abounds that US relations severed since 1959 may get mended again. The Washington-Havana axis stops in Miami, for now only politicians trekking between capitals and come election time, ready to cash-in on their earned Cuban political capital. A sad chapter in Chile unraveled late this year, unforgotten war wounds wide open with tears. Former President General Pinochet lived to live his shame, hiding his last years from the vengeful relatives seeking to even the game.

Throughout the Middle East and resurrected from an earlier time comes again the spirit of Saladin and his apocalypse on the Crusaders, the centuries in between only a blimp on the horizon of modern day religion traders. Wars have since taken new extremes: the assault is made with caricatures on religions and the revered, the war on the hijab one veiled theme. The Crystal Ball can see it all in a grand scheme, as the beauty world fears the drop in sales of all products cosmetic and hair colorings, how to sell when the lips are veiled and the hair is under chastity coverings.

Turkey is knocking on the European Union while the Pope is trying to unlock the keys to the re-union, a gallant effort to redeem his blemished Islamic world esteem. Whether it was a slip of the pen or a historical glitch from fifteenth century ages, he came under heat and much scrutiny for words some deemed unbecoming of The Holy See. The island of Cyprus remains the lock and the key as a member of the Common Union, Turkey the only would-be of a different communion.

At the UN action was loud as talk of evils and devils rocked the stage of the worldwide forum. The US Congress booted out UN Ambassador Bolton the scratch man as a farewell gift to the UN's chief Kofi Annan. From Korea comes the next pin, patiently awaiting the approval of the new boss from the host of the UN. Jimmy Carter is headlines again making a last ditch effort at Middle East Peace, and trying to pin the elusive legacy as the man who made The Peace. The prize was at hand when he engineered the historic union, only to slip away into oblivion. The much talked about barter of the time remains an unfulfilled dream of President Carter to redress the two world wars wounds and crimes.

Italy, home of the enchanting Turin 2006 Winter Olympics and where love is always is in the air, is once again having a limelight romance with actors parading castles in wedding gowns, Tom Cruise and his bride romancing the town. The blue blood royals of yesteryear are warily eyeing the Jumping Jack Flash on Oprah's couch, Mick Jagger stealing her TV show to springboard his next movie show. The Soaps where out there in full force with eager Paparazzi always in search of a new media power horse ever since Diana passed on the torch. In Hollywood a monster is at the ticket box: hot and all the rage James Bond is back, in his women pursuits and heroic attacks.

The Asian Games of 2006 were hosted by the always-generous Qatar, grand and sumptuous with an Arabian stallion making the long climb to light the torch by his rider. In Dubai the leap into the future has already taken place, time is in a wrap on the former empty plains constrained only by the shortage of cranes to lift up more skyscraper cranes, and to propel the optimistic mind gears to higher planes.

War has been good to Dow and Jones, terrorism and the scare a boon to the US bond market. Peace may not have a dividend if the foreign holders thereafter dump US financial instruments. Also this year in the US, normally a field of dreams, the chase turned the game into a political minefield. A game of hunter and hunted, with hunters ferociously and rigorously scouting the hunted, Democrats came pounding and Republicans were howling, their ranks splitting far and wide with politicos bailing out to save their hide. An icon of sorts unraveled this year: with the stock market at an all time high, unemployment at an all time low, inflation near zero and interest rates near historic lows, the November elections should have been sewed up. "It's the economy stupid" unraveled and crumbled down at the ballot box, ending twelve years of Republican rule and tumbling many incumbents off the rocks.

At the November elections and by Thanksgiving,

the Democrats had their duck lame after the final vote count and fuss and games, and the consequences for the rich are beware. The end of passing your estate and highlife non-taxable may become real, as the Democrats zero-in on the Estate Tax Law repeal. You may skip the coming slaughter and still savor your fine wines if you time your exit to the "next life" by 2009.

A couple of years forward and for the US presidential elections of 2008 some of the horses are already out of the gate. The show is a must win for every horse as Senator Hillary eyes her ultimate career course. Paving the way ahead of the pack is her former First Lady title as she parades exuberantly on the saddle. At the end of the brawl and if it comes to be, and she carries the day despite Speaker Pelosi, a new name will have to be found for a past president par excellence, the First Lady Ladies Man.

Over the years state governors have unseated incumbents and many aspiring congressmen for president, their chances better without the baggage of a congressional voting record. Presidents Bush, Clinton, Reagan and Carter made the leap to the top of the heap, many of the high and seemingly mighty swept under the seat. Capable, cool and collected, Governor Perry of Texas has been christened again for a new term, his seat the springboard that launched the White House present head. History provides no clue for same State Governor-to-President back-to-back, a challenging feat when it is getting steeper to climb the incumbent's track.

Nature took a tame course this year, save for a few fires to remind us of the lurking potential. Hurricanes also had a break after twisting and twirling all last year. While ice appears melting at the North Pole, the southern Argentina glacier ice is gaining. Will the increased weight of the ice mass change the azimuth by a few degrees, topple the globe and flip flop global warming on its heals?

Construction started on The Freedom Tower in lower Manhattan to raise the spirit high above the mischief of 9-11. And for the first time the US population passed the three hundred million mark. Lucky for us water was just discovered on planet Enceladus, if we can only set-up shop on Saturn to explore its sixth sibling.

As New Orleans was abandoned to its vices, still caught between the flood and a tiny dry space, Houston continues to settle in, digesting the hurricanes of last year and their aftermath. Some Louisiana flair remains in the air though tempers flare when government is about to end their welfare. Houston is on an urban infill and suburban quest leaving no patches skipped, tightening the noose around the stretched out necks seeking deals and still dreaming of steals. Desirable lots are like aged beef and wine, Choice and selling at Prime. In Downtown Houston the Florida-Pacific interstate intertwines with the Mexico-Maine inter-connect, at times creating a challenging bottleneck. Both are swirling and twirling and going into hoops and loops, loop upon loop. The Grand Parkway Loop, now in chops, has mapped The Taking, pastures and farmlands only short stops for the Eminent Domain acquisition powers to carry this huge undertaking.

High Tech obliged Man well this year. First came TOTO with the ultimate "Toilet Bidet Combo", heated, energized and "sensorized", computer chips doing all the tricks. Man's new best friend is no animal, and with only air power to flush, the water-less urinal is flashing on the ace a Royal Flush.

As we reach the 2006 end of the line, may the world continues to spread bounty and beauty upon everyone, and hopefully each of us in their special way will always step up to the line and do what was always handed down by the elders of time, and all the newer divines. Enjoy every moment of time, have a happy new year, and until next time.

Imad F. Abdullah, December 2006

The Year 2005

2005 WAS UNQUESTIONABLY THE YEAR of Hurricanes.

War, the bird flu, and earthquakes, all tried to capture this year in vain, but with much destruction to spare, the title was won handily by the flood masters of the plains. Hurricanes Rita and Katrina were outdoing their upstart sisters, choosing their targets with vindictiveness and precision, and vying for the highest book of records position. Old Man Sea called from the deep, "it's mine to take, not yours to keep".

Disaster came high from the sky, fierce and spread out, and a spinning wheel of misfortune. The celestial bowls stranded millions on highways everywhere with fuel to nowhere. New Orleans, the home of Sugar and the Pro-Bowl, was turned into a deep mud hole, a wasteland the Biblical has not foretold. Amassed masses wept in the dark in vain hopes of rescue by Noah Ark. Under the weight and action of salt water and chemical waste the soils were pulverizing, and with no more living space the city's tax base was vaporizing. The environmental Holocaust caused so many everything to lose, that even Jazz was weeping as it could not keep up with that many Blues.

Many a Jack hit the road, never to come back no more no more. How to govern without people, when power is from the people and to the people, as the flood fare-welled the remnants of people?

In Texas where superlatives are normal pastime, Houston faced the challenge of a lifetime, staring at a sea-monster aiming to swallow back his personal oil wealth, nature's way to lubricate its engine of destruction and death. The monster blinked at the last few hours, choosing instead a lesser foe on an easterly path, and slowly but edgily life returned to normalcy. What to do next year if a hurricane gets near? As the land of oil and refinery rows could not deliver the gas tankers to the stranded exodus on the roads, will everyone pack up their town or brave the collapsing dams in lieu of the traffic jams?

With such an opportune time the rising crescendo of global warming is warning that glaciers are melting and seas are rising. Low on corporate balance sheets, Kyoto is high on the list of Greenpeace claiming emissions cut down the ozone greenhouse lease. Celestial holes are getting bigger pending a behavioral evolution, and temperatures are upwards inching us into oblivion.

Climate change winners and losers abound as new farmland could sprout in former desert sands. CO_2 grows trees faster than just oxygen, and more evaporation spreads rainfall to the arid and wasted, and creates new bread baskets. Touting 2025 or 2050, definitely by 3,000 when we'll all bake or worse yet freeze our hair, how to sort the seas with an inch rise here and there as the one Fahrenheit will make us shiver in despair. Coastal cities are chasing land inland while Venice rakes in loads of money from all who want a piece of the Medici, before saying Ciao and sinking to the sea. Real or unreal, true or hype, warm-up to the concept as warming hypes its onset.

2005 was also a year of reconciliation for the great divide, between both red and blue continents of the divide and the intercontinental dissent worldwide. Soft spoken, cool and collected, Secretary of State Condi is roaming the world bartering peace far and wide, knowing she's got the baddest obedience stick worldwide. The world is in turmoil as the culprit remains the elusive oil, standing tall with every pricing overhaul.

The Soviet Block, now in chips, is being played on various poker tables, counting change and stacking the deck for the next and lukewarm East West political storm. North Korea anchors one end, Iran is troubleshooting another end, and the former Eastern European block buffers the invasion of the always-suspicious globalization. China is on the rise and India is chasing its own sunrise. Techs in India are 24-7 on call, standby operators giving computech advice with courtesy and zealous drive.

Communist only in name, China plugs along amassing greenbacks in billions and looking for industrial trophies worldwide. Much is still to do in China, the race between humanity and prosper-

ity a daily battle at full speed. Prospects look good
if Shanghai is a model, urban capitalism above and
underground soaring high and deep, all built on peo-
ple-leased land awaiting patiently the return of all
fixed assets to the motherland. Shanghai is a stunning
feat in so few years and a great delight, showcasing
China in the limelight. Olympics 08 in Beijing are on
the way, and the torch is already shining the light all
the way. Not to be left behind, Hong Kong is touting
its horn with the opening of the new Disneyland.

In Iraq they're daily butting heads, and the Middle
East peace remains elusive buttressed by hardheads
and knuckleheads. Syria is frequently in the headlines, being pushed to lower its hemlines. Iran and
Syria are in the crosshairs, with so much chatter
filling the air. Iran is on the atomic bandwagon trying
to best the West by evading the atomic test, enrich-
ing their Uranium is spreading scares and causing
concerned stares. For Iran's old foe, the Mother of
all Trials just began, surviving plaintiffs packing the
accusing line in the hunt for Iraq's President Saddam.
More Trials of the Century will be surely be dubbed
in time, pending the TV ratings of their un-ceasing
nighttime anchors thriving on selling stories of crime.

A shocking blast in Beirut took the life of Prime
Minister Rafik Hariri and several of the entourage in
one hellish criminal act. It all happened in a flash but
the fallout and repercussions are bound to change
political alliances and ignite sectarian discussions.

Always on trial is President Bush as Hollywood
moguls and Democrats are pulling together and
finger pointing for the upcoming election push. Re-

elected ready and president already starting this year, his speeches are custom tailored for optimism, look-ahead vision and realism. A new U.S. kingpin is at the U.N. pushing to get votes and mobilize with his Cross- Pen. The Supreme Court was big news for who would get the honor to replace Sandra Day O'Connor. From apprentice to chief justice, John G. Roberts, Jr. made the career leap in no time winning conservatives for life preservation in a Congress bent on consternation.

America's demographics keep changing. Marriage is confused with same sex worship, when two such halves are applicants for partnership. Love is sidelined while candidates check the significance of their other as credit and scores, and the new bank-ruptcy laws are giving them ample reason to pause before the close. Marriage is considering incorporat-ing, splitting shares based on the credit score and the power of borrowing, eternal love barely leveraging.

The bellowing smoke from the Vatican early this year signaled a new Pope, the venerable Archbish-ops giving fresh hope after the legacy of the late Jean Paul Pope. Churches could be running out of space as the Lakewood Church in Houston is already hosting Fifteen Grand worshipers a sermon at the former basketball Summit turned Holy Kingdom. As the faithful multiply in search of more heavenly space, churches are booking more of the available multi-plex entertainment place. At the movie theaters on Sunday morning the sermon has an extra time slot, filling all the shoppers hitherto parking lots. And for the children and in time, they may have cartoon sermons to make believe little Sam in lieu of the original run of the mill cartoons of Shazam and his every subsequent acrobat man.

In another sect, an almost perennial financial religion, stock worshippers remain eager enthusiasts praying to catch the lows for the ultimate highs. Their chapel of capital on Wall Street is well attended 5 days a week, with pundits giving sermons all the while in fancy style professing foresight on how to catch heaven on a rising star and to uplift fortunes by hanging to gold bars.

While Microsoft treads water and GM clunks and drags along a back-breaking retirement fund, the young and strong Google is leaping ahead toward the zillion and gobbling along the way smaller fish and a host of whales worth billions. The stock markets this year were not much below par, as interest rates inch up across the rate bar, at the helm a new Fed Czar. The dollar is forging ahead as countries still hoard dollar instruments without yet much dread and Europe is getting cheaper on the Yankee spread. Consumers are paying for gas through the nose and the United States deficit is driving the spending as the worldwide economy grows. More gadgets than anyone could fathom are coming on line all the time, if only we have the time to get them working online.

You Tube hit the tube this year in plenty time to watch the re-runs of the low-key wedding of British Prince Charles and Camille. Many fans worldwide remained glued to the tube until California courts acquitted pop star Michael Jackson on trial for a molestation charge.

Cities continue their outward explosion into suburban pastures, freeways in pursuit, with anti-crawlers always a threat as anti-growth prowlers. Cities breed cities and towns as the natural order continues the sprawl, in the absence of cities birth control. Houston wingtips are spreading wide, dream prices are coming true as land is getting scarce, and the push is everywhere chasing land previously nowhere. In town the lofts command a lofty price, loftier the higher you go up in the air, while the claimed housing bubble remains full of hot air.

As Houston opened the doors wide for hurricane evacuees, it became a model of corporate largesse and rarely seen organization among public entities. Thereafter our Mayor was re-elected for a second term by the highest of margins for any incumbent ever to run. Houston continues the quest for a City, hybrid as it is, split between the in-crowd die-hards and the car-oriented week-enders braving commuting by blasting music hard. Superimposed by rail, toll and more Loops, it's a constant conflict between private car and public transport as Rail and Toll cut through like a double-edged sword, slicing at times inconsistently and mercilessly. Toll roads are feeding more such ways and finding new ways to toll making everyone work harder and toil. The debate continues, a real democracy of real estate at work.

As computers mature and hardware becomes house ware, our shopping patterns are altering our wares and wears. Life is getting faster with the Internet, going around the world in a flash from our own bed. With viruses attached for computer deconstruction, Spam is the new weapon of mass destruction. In spite of it all, dedication is still everywhere, commitments abound and the world shall prosper and survive. On the family front we celebrated our son Sammy's graduation from the University of Texas last May, and he's now a happy camper working in Downtown Houston for pay.

Well said once upon a time, "friendships are better than wine as they always are maturing, and you can never drink enough from those left on the vine". Thank you for the friendship all these years, enjoy the season and be merry while adding seasonal pounds, a new year is upon us with many merry-go-rounds. Let our love be crystal clear, and until the New Crystal next year, have a happy new year.

Imad F. Abdullah, December 2005

The Year 2004

2004 HAS BEEN A YEAR of superlatives.

Much has happened this past year, with a new dawn for one reigning US President, and a farewell to a past President. With a perfectly gallant funeral America bid farewell to the much beloved President Reagan and as he rode into the sunset, his legacy was a reminder that new dawns can always shine, and if we can all rise collectively we can make many Suns rise.

And we witnessed the search for eternal fame celebrated under the perennial flame. It was a new age of Olympianship as they all headed to Athens after the gods of ancient Greece, hoping their grace will produce them a championship. The Goddesses are still there both in stone and flesh and the monuments stand out on the Hill, The Parthenon still the majestic dream

Though the Olympics in Greece produce heroes of Sport at Athena's Forums, a new breed of Olympians were competing under a new decorum where the champ would rule the world: presidential debates featured a different breed of gladiators, masters at the art of weaving and weaseling through pointed questions and unsavory situations.

04 was a year of election frenzy with John Kerry's past locking his future, and no veep able to unlock his fortunes. The guess who dunnit and "who where did when" filled the air. American nationalism was fought over the waves snatching the red and the blue out of the coveted flag, leaving behind only strings of white and very few stars.

While Republicans draped in red, Democrats cast their lot in blue and the leftover democracy was wrapped with remnants of the stars and stripes. In normal times they reside side by side in peaceful respect on the flag but today they have gone astray worlds apart. Republican "ism" sprayed the mid lands in red and the Demos "tism" spread the blue at both ends. A continent with a wide divide spilled red over the blue waters at each end leaving the blues singing The Blues to no end.

In "Point and Counterpoint" Republicans would say: ask not what Government can do for me, ask government to let it be. Democrats also have their say: give me your tired, give me your poor, hand me your votes and I will tax the over-blessed to keep your old age secure.

2008 is upon us already, some 1400 days away give or take and counting. All eyes are fixated on the softer half of one super Democrat turned librarian in Little Rock with the opening of his presidential library. Republicans already know who'll be the foe and they're searching for a missing ace to ace the deck again. In their search they are toying with a former Hollywood superstar turned a Californian czar, in hopes of beating Hillary Clinton to the Hill with the world champ Schwarzenegger as a powerful swinger at the par.

If California's coveted votes can be had, the Electoral College can turn upside down. Constitutional changes are no easy task but they could switch some minds around, and help to line up a candidate's lucky stars. Mobilizing Hollywood is no easy task as expensive stardom has its' price and political stands make and break careers overnight.

If all else fails the 43rd president Bush can get a new vice president midway, make an exchange, retire VP Dick Cheney and prep another seasoned face, a she who would have to balance the challenge of the Democratic ticket with a pretty face. Yet as Hillary ponders a Vice without vice, who would have thought Senator Edwards for Vice President would be smothered by fellow Carolinians piling up the heap. Evermore is the importance of selecting a solid vice president, not so much for oratory skills or good looks or for making money by legal hoops.

The next Democrat Veep on the slate will need to carry at least one pivotal state. Better stay off the Hollywood trail and go for a seasoned governor of a large state where his local record will not haunt the whole slate.

Even Hollywood religion has passionately left its mark, raising millions for one Mel Gibson for-profit megastar, a lucky Catholic on a mission to further his movie "The Passion" about the most revered holy star.

Another befitting way to describe 2004 can be summed up in one word: Crude.

As gruesome and crude fighting continues in Iraq, the real crude awakening was quite shocking to say the least, jumping to $55 per barrel before the catch-your-breath retreat. As the cost of printing money for this war is going overboard, black oil lived up to its name as the indispensable yellow gold. From a land where race is yellow but almost gold, the Renminbi followed suit and acted bold, sending a clear signal: the Euro has arrived as the one to hold.

And in Florida this could have been classed as the year of super hurricanes, brutally ravaging creatures of rude character, blowing and looting with no mercy time and again, reminders of a nature unkind playing havoc with the destiny of mankind. Disaster did not spare Southeast Asia as the 9.1 magnitude earthquake jolted the sea waves and sent the tsunami in its wake on a wild and brutal trek: 230,000 perished.

Worldwide a super basket case is developing for the whole continent of Africa. Still waiting on foreign aid Africa is being savaged by AIDS, an unforgiving disease spreading like wildfire. Sudan is frequently in the headlines and Darfur continues to scramble for the yet to arrive Petit Four. Shades of a British Queen of yesteryear concerned about how to get the hungry fed: "Let them eat Cake if there is no bread".

And to The Middle East where the action never stops, 24 hours of daily excitement mixed in with flesh and bones. Iraq is powder everywhere, keg at times, dusty all the times. Crude is again slowly flowing in pipelines, every now and then made to protrude over ravines and ancient palms and pending resolution of new elections to spread the much anticipated calm.

Iraq, the land of the original Khalifats and the now jailed President Saddam famous for his sword act, is looking to elect a majority "All-ism" for a multitude of "Sectaniarianisms", to embrace all the sects and religious "isms". January's the deadline to stop the bloodshed and the heinous crimes.

Much noble intent engulfed the elusive Middle East peace, that even laureates of Nobel lent their hands to piece it piece by piece. Oslo became famous over its secret "Accords" and Camp David came to life with all the give and take offers. Take it or leave aside, many still died while the elusive quest remains hollow inside. Come others now on the scene, past, present and future collide, leaders unable still to put differences aside. A presidential legacy can still be had, one that eluded Presidents Reagan, Carter, Clinton, and Bush the father and son so far.

Nobility has never been his claim but Nobel gave him fame. Some saw Palestinian leader Yasser Arafat as the bearded shadowy face looming over peace upheavals, others see his Nobel prize mixed-in with unsavory deeds. Never has there been such love-hate rhetoric over forty years with a personality deemed so historic. Nobel was unable to forestall destiny and Arafat passed away to his next life journey.

With Arafat passing away on the last day of the holy month of Ramadan, maybe the prayers to Mecca had just the sign. In Mecca itself the Hajj remains the

anchor of Islam's faith, the Holy City a restful place
for the souls of the pilgrims trampled to death in a
frenzied stampede while fulfilling their faith.

In another western Mecca known as a gamblers
paradise, the stock markets operate in a surreal
fashion and look for clues in every tavern. The Wall
of the Street rose uninterrupted for the whole time
since Arafat left his hometown until his demise. His
followers claimed it as a sign of the divine, but the
Street gamblers know better that this new rise may
only be a passing surprise.

Turbulent Wall Street times can still be ahead and
the logistics of the crude are bound to spin prices and
swindle many investing heads. Riding high on a SUV
seat is getting costlier with each mile. The markets
were unpredictable this year with elections hovering
always near. Google got golden and the Euro is
flexing, but Europe was seen as vexing. The dailies
always have to do the hype otherwise readership
will take a hike. Large market makers follow trends
and waves, chart points, and seasonal moves based
on historical trends. Movers and shakers follow the
Stock Market Almanac and they have large amounts
to position in many stocks at one time. Whereas we
have to pick and choose and be right on timing all the
time, they can play golf for a pastime.

Two giants of retail became one this year, Kmart
gobbling rival Sears for eleven billion and retaining
the historical and revered name as Sears Holding.
Another giant of cyberspace launched "gmail" but
many thought it foul play as it started on April 1st,
fools day.

America's new Prime-Time is extended criminal trials, filling the airwaves with experts and text perverts, and would be advisers and "expertenacious" interpreters. The soaring ratings after the infamous and controversial O. J. Simpson trial, gave the media new superstars to fill the time, and to capitalize on the ratings in case of his potential demise, insuring sparks and fireworks if the ending is on the capital punishment device. Who's next for 2005 and which new and improved and preposterous crime is bound to capture the media advertising minds? Though "Oldsmobile" was killed it doesn't qualify but maybe the yet to be super crime to go head-to-head with "Sex and the City" is already in the pipeline waiting for the zealous reportage.

Too much hype nowadays in the news but very little substance gets diffused. Knowledge is a two-edged sword, but with no underhanded secrecy it may be detrimental to a successful democracy. They might as well fill the airwave time with soap and sports as they require less integrity. We're fed so much junk with all the insignificant pundit views that we know all about nothing when it comes to worthy news.

And with his career dented during elections by a news act and rather than getting hammered by the facts, Dan Rather chose to get off the tracks. He is retiring happily from his work and kissing goodbye his network. It's time to write a book and get on the speakers list and explore history with Larry King at no risk.

Architecture continues to soar to new heights as the "Taipei 101" skyscraper became the world's tallest one. On the home front, Houston continues on a fascinating rampage, gobbling central and peripheral real estate at an incredulous speed. Typical alarmists are sounding the horns of disappearing Real Estate under the weight of ever greedy speculators, and the would-be thieves of the serenity of farm land all over the State. The owners of the fields are getting rich and living in peace as the engines of developers maintain the economy at high speed, and extend the reach for capital to Houston worldwide and overseas.

As if literally embarking on water, several cruise lines with "Super-Queens" are vying for international destinations and treating tourists as kings and queens, her RMS Queen Mary 2 christened by Her Majesty Elizabeth II, the ultimate queen.

Early in the year Houston was host to many stars, when we all came for the Super bowl together at heart, Republican and Democrats. Houston raised the bar on the class with our sparkling new light-rail to both ends of Midtown. Excitement abounds for future spreads and politicos are plugging their wants for extension rail lines and forging ahead. With super speed and a different power train, NASA elevated our spirits with the landing on Mars of its rover aptly named "Spirit".

A new mayor for Houston is at the helm, the honorable Bill White replaced the term-limited Mayor Lee Brown. All eyes are now on City Hall, how he will handle the budget shortfall. Another superlative dawned on Houston as the first Hispanic school district superintendent is facing his super-sized mandate, and a challenging and over-sized drop-out rate. His annual super compensation package of nearly half a million dollars is raising eyebrows and is food for thought at the next round of property tax hike cries.

As 2005 peaks on us, clouds and rays, and howls and growls, capitalism is alive and well, and at times naked bare. The Catholic Church is in deep despair, as the magic is wearing off cathedrals and spires with all the accusation of improper sex affairs. A breed apart, re-elected #43 is in saddle again, and along with western and cowboys, we're riding the next four years with a Texas home boy. The wagons are loaded with the weight of past years, and the horses are feeling it with overloaded gears. Forward we go, can't go back, as the challenges will always make a comeback. Best wishes and happy warm and joyful holidays to you from Texas, and until next year.

Imad F. Abdullah, December 2004, Houston, Texas.

The Year 2003

2003 STARTED AS THE YEAR of Democracy but ended up being the year of the Spider Hole.

It was a turbulent year on the whole: the stock markets snapped back after a big fall, the dollar is still sinking whole but the euro is singing "Glory to All." Saddam is out of the hole and now headed to the justice hall, and his $750,000 is one big loot to haul.

North Korea is playing hardball, a World Series game of atomic proportions with nukes for baseballs.

The year 2003 has also been "a year in waiting," though no one knew for what. The UN is on standby waiting for a green light that's still on yellow. The weapons of mass destruction are nowhere to be found and the underground is swelling the Iraqi grounds, with some still desperately hanging for "sisterhood" with Vietnam. Many Iraqis roam the land hoping to be around when it's time to share their life stories with siblings of today's playground.

On the Western front a relic of the past is raising its mast: "The Draft" is looming large as America is running short of its best lot with not enough soldiers under arms to fill shoes in the shifty sands of Iraq and Afghanistan, a drying pipeline for the coveted pipelines.

The volunteer draft is searching for reservists to serve the Flag, and the young upstarts are scrambling to grow older and age quicker to beat any deadline for the race in the Desert Drag. Watch out if you're eighteen or thereabouts; Iraq may become your history if you're called to pack, and if you're lucky to march out and come back.

Elections are already upon us for next year, once again with numerous junior stars looking to unseat the present Czar. Democracy breeds candidates from everywhere: Congressmen and past generals and governors are aspiring alike, many in it for a vice-presidential stake, hopeful and vying for a run to the home plate.

While they analyze and opinionate with authority, a wiser Hillary is holding back on running a horse to the White House, leaving the Democrats to their fate in case it becomes "Slaughter House". For her plenty of time is left for '08 when no incumbents are in sight and Republicans would be spent fighting past and upcoming wars. The Clinton Mystique may work the charm of the spouse and scrutiny will reign on "aides" in the White House.

Which Democrat will survive to go in overdrive after the lengthy marathon weeds out the pack to face the entrenched White House tribe, and to spearhead the Democrats on the Grand Prix Drive? Still too early for the surprise

What will be the game ten months from now
to mobilize all the clan? Will it be "the economy
stupid" or the stock market decline, maybe another
mini 9/11, or the mysterious Bin Laden whereabouts?
Will "Homeland Un-security" be the plan and what
platform if they hope to unseat the man? Too many
uncertain times but unemployment and China and
Korea will be in line for the headlines. To help out
and at the gate, a Hollywood mogulette: Barbara
Streisand is trying to play roulette on the candidate
who can win a "Texas Hold 'em poker charrette".

Greenspan remains at the helm holding the rein
on interest rates, stretching dollars and minting
presses for new ones and playing the loyalty game
in an election year. Inflation is tame while housing
is on a tear, sucking the middle class cash for down
payments. The future "weekend fix-it" slaves are
happier than ever, their future now running with the
land. On the whole and while people in other countries save more since more rent than own, Americans
continue buying houses to build equity and living
smart, while spending the rest of the paycheck at the
typical sucking-marts.

Capitalism is built up on the back of savings.
Liquidity abounds for now and rates are low but
headed to the unknown. Every guru says "nowhere
but up" yet stubbornly low they remain. Sooner or
later it will be true, whether many years down the
line or before November 2004. The Crystal Ball envisions June or July of '04.

Deficits are back, a gift from Iraq. The tech bust
redeemed itself but only for those who were in.

The euro is flexing muscle, up while the dollar is a tagalong. The yellow metal shines as gold is pampering the $400 mark after years of rest and relaxation.

It was year three of a typical US administration also known as "pre-presidential," the year before the election. History had a guarantee of market upturn running for sixty-four years continuously. History repeated itself again following the same trend line. With the fine art of presidential manipulation and true to the same logic, stocks in '03 are up through the sixty-fifth year and rewarding the faithful who play strategic.

"Market Up" as it is shown on charts is a function of the Dow Jones being priced in vanishing US dollars. Flat it becomes when value on the chart is shown in Euro or gold, at times trending down in surreal style.

In another time the different stages of market downturns and recovery were observed in the 1500s by a renowned author of his time. After he's seen hell and turmoil with the markets and got in the know, rumor has it he wrote his famous "Dante's Inferno".

From the West and in California, Santa Ana was no Santa this year, coming much earlier than Christmas ShowTime and howling and growling through hills and ravines, devouring houses and spreading fire through trees. For those escaping from Los Angeles going east, whether from fires or to buy cheap, a sparkling place unfolds and if you play cards it's best to fold. Las Vegas is on a roll and on unlucky gamblers taking its toll. Fire or flood can be tamed but rolling the dice for most is an effort in vain.

Back to the beginning and reminiscing about a

future yet to be, Democracy is saddled with draw-backs as it softens resolve and turns might into "tigerless paper resolutions." Democracy every now and then needs to stiffen its tone and only the fanatics can deliver a backbone. Be it Muslim Right or Christian Right, lessons are learned from another time and another place, shades of crusading marauders when "the swordly ways" united empires and kingdoms. Resolve is not necessarily fair but "Homeland Security" is determined to keep it there with many former friendships lingering in despair.

Democracy comes in models much like cars: the "for export" model is different from "domestic" which benefits from the US Constitution and the Electoral College guaranteeing majority rule. The exported model guarantees "minority scramble to rule" and keeps busy bodies in search of universal rules. Conflict begins internal and anarchy takes over "Democracy's Copyright," and it could spill over.

Japan is rising again slowly but surely and Afghanistan is becoming history, no longer worthy of news. It's cheaper this way as the first eighty seven billion dollars for Iraq is draining the will of Congress to spread more billions and display more largesse.

As continents collide, the third and fourth world wars occur now on faraway lands while the Axis and the Allies battle it over the spoils of contracts. As jobs are lost here and there, countries are losing jobs to lesser neighboring fares. There is always a hungrier frère and even China is losing manufacturing jobs to neighboring countries, an everlasting supply of exploitation laissez-faire.

Back again to the hole, a new fight looms big in New York about the Manhattan hellish Hole: how to make another "Holy Wall" for so much pilgrimage to the memorial hall. Architects and developers collide, the pride mixed with the money sound. The 9/11 Memorial will be the topic of next year, how to make money with respect for the counted and the still-missing heads, when the highest tower is planned over the memories of the dead.

A new kid is in town from another almost-island foreign land: the Al-Jazeera network is butting heads on airwaves already saturated with titans in control for many decades and where pundits on the air are talking heads know it all after all, and with their claimed facts feeding the noisy chatter sprawl.

On our home front much has happened last year. Houstonians voted to build more rail and we're all waiting to ride the train come January 1. Another new transformation is taking shape at a former home for the stars, from superstars to aspiring stars: the Astrodome may be converted to a home for the faraway megastars, a museum and fantasyland for space above the stars.

And now that we moved from one Astrodome and built a double dome, Houston is hosting the Super Bowl in the new dome where gladiators will carve a name in search of eternity on a wall, in the Hall of Fame of football.

The former basketball arena with fading memories of winning play-offs and seasons is being transformed again for new reasons: after a stunt as Compaq Center driven by the power of advertising, the previous beloved Summit as it was called is now being converted to a House of the Lord, a 15,000-seat non-denominational spectacle with starry eyes coming from afar, chanting hymns and gazing towards the Ultimate Star.

Another fame for all is in store in '04 as the Olympics in Athens get near and a new airport is in gear. A precision German-built toll road leads to the Parthenon, a dream come true from the days when roaming Spartans victoriously marched on.

Adding more entries to our memories our family travels took us this year to Italy, an enchanting land with incredible history. We left Speed Limit at home, and raced the ways and winding roads to Venice and Pisa where the leaning tower is still holding its own, and to Florence and its dome: David is still there, a true glory of stone.

And after many years in anticipation, we visited the lands of the Far East with wonderful friends in Tokyo and Hong Kong for a phenomenal touristic treat and great dining feasts. They're the future in experiments of urban solutions to mass density, fabulous places by all means with subways below and up high with trains and freeway spines elevated through buildings and canyons and rims.

As we peek in on the new year in less than two, and maybe one week, the Crystal Ball is forward looking, hedging options on Futures and making stock bets on where markets head and what waves are ahead, and depending on whether a new horse will be riding the herd instead. Candidates are still scrambling from near and far in search of votes and marketing bread. It doesn't look too bad though the ratings for most are still dread, but once upon a time and crisscrossing this land, a Georgia resident went around: "My name is Jimmy Carter and I am running for president." Few heeded his plan but he still rules the *Larry King Live* on the airwaves every now and then.

The new names are now in the hat, same troubadours looking to fill a larger-than-life cowboy hat. Whether up or down it looks to be a choppy ride, ugly for some but sweet to the one, when it's all said and done. Time to keep your saddles straight and hold on to the rope, and best wishes to you from Texas for an '04 winning horse.

Imad F. Abdullah, December 2003

The Year 2002

2002 WAS THE YEAR OF the aftermath.

TwoZeroZeroTwo will be remembered for two zeroed-out towers that dominated the year in eternal fame and spirit. Only a hollow hole is left from the whole that even Halloween is petrified within the hallowed walls. May a hell on earth open the gates of heaven to embrace the victims of scarred Manhattan.

This has also been a year in limbo: limbo on war, limbo for when, and limbo at the UN, to go or not to go. Limbo now is slow, on the go.

Not much known to begin the cheer about this coming year, yet two wars this century are already history: goodbye Taliban and sayonara Slobodan. North Korea and Iraq are on the plate, waiting in queue for a clue, and maybe a new blockbuster from Hollywood will improve the view. Wars are cliff-hangers for real, a very tough spot for the lead role of the reel. We'll find out early next year, how it turns and how it steers, more likely after the football bowls since we still need to cheer. After the Super Bowl could be a time for the stormy brawl.

Democracy is in great pain nowadays: back then, the US Constitution banked on the inherent conflict between the Presidency, Congress, and an independent press, to maintain checks and balances. The press and the White House are in line for now, and the Supreme Court is loaded to keep Laws fair. Congress is scrambled in its affairs and fresh Congress members are aimless not understanding how or where, and why in decisions they can't share.

Looking ahead through muddy waters and all, the Crystal Ball will peak into the future and try to make sense of the calls: a medley of clouds on the horizon, and oil spikes in store. The Stock Market whip-lashes and saws are slashing funds with nasty claws. If you're looking for a cue, all the Q's are splintered factions: IraQ is waiting for a reaction, Al Qaeda is in temporary inaction, and the Nasdaq QQQ Index is full of action. A Gulf War in the streets can have lives at stake, but every day war on Wall Street can claim your Steak.

If you're out of the markets for now and fat, it's time to nibble in, but if you're in but slim, catch the pops periodically and cash in: better some than none. These are not the times for the mutual funds faithful at heart or the perennial optimist on the long term charts: this is the trading time, day in day out, in and out. Play it close on the Shorts and Longs, keep your money at bay, and hedge precious funds away.

It could be a difficult year, with inflation and deflation fighting it out. Deflation is high because money is cheap. Inflation is low since the cost index keeps too many items out of the heap, and because the income of government employees is tied to the index creep. Government tries not to go broke faster than necessary, at least until they change the formula and retire us at 72. It's getting close...

The continuous increases of contribution limits to your retirement plans are feeding the frenzy of market sharks. With continuous losses, the young still have the next thirty years for an upside. For the retired or soon to be, it's time to plan your coming out of retirement party. Hold on to your IRA, before it goes the IRAQ way.

The Key to market success is to continually climb the ladder of information: the higher we get, the more we need to climb, and the faster we must try to get there. Most important, after we get there, is how to interpret and sort it out square. The Pros claim to do it fulltime, shady claims in the best of times, and with fine print disclaimers in the worst of times.

For an insider tip on how to be the first to know, first hand, the production and manufacturing direction, and with the best and most reliable indicator for when markets go Bull, (no bull), check the stats of cardboard box makers. When their orders increase, American Industry is shipping out, and the cash flow follows straight up.

Now that we're compounding to get rich in the safety heaven of the two percent savings accounts and would be three percent inflation (negative math anyway), beware of the hidden equipment upgrade inflation and costs necessary to stay ahead of stagnation.

In the race to save time, a New Generation is

taking shape, across ageless generations and throughout the nation: we've all become wired wizards with
much pizzazz, and this "Z Generation" is here to zip
and zap: give us computers, gives us Palm, give us
Laps and give us Tops, give us flat screens and give
us voice streams. Wire us forward, and zap it on our
extra loaded Plastic, just extend the payment plan…

In search of inspiration and looking ahead for
new architectural wonders, the newest museum
of the wandering and once technology's wonders
is shaping up. In California and hot and dry, the
Mohave Desert Plane Museum is buzzing with Plane
Art, all in not out, celebrating this new migration of
sonic birds, to be mothballed waiting for better times
to head again skywards. Maybe the third world will
amass enough money to buy, if they ever close the
gap. The end of the line is here for much of the fleet,
united they stand in the misery of the times.

Speaking of United, the "unionited" bossy stands
busted UAL Airlines, a living proof that employees
as owners can run the profits out of business plans.
Ten cents on the dollar is what's left, with ten yards a
mile, for our sky miles.

The Skies have never been un-friendlier: keep
your scissors at bay and your nail cutters inside, better
yet send them ahead by Fed-Ex lest you're arrested
by the zealots at the airport waiting line. Make your
home a sweet home, these are driving times.

Houston is already in good times with $25 oil.
A War on Iraq could fuel Houston's economy as oil
services will be in demand to upgrade and re-work
Iraq's Facilities. Houston could go on a run with oil

companies going to map and mop and re-rack the impending leftover war cracks of Iraq.

And Houston's football is in new stadium stands, with the Texans at "Four and O", no matter the loosing count. Everyone is flashing smiles and beams, as 4 wins first year is no easy feat for an expansion team.

Texas on the whole gets high and on a roll with high oil, producing black gold and presidential timber. Texas is renowned for exporting its high-powered politicians to Washington, keeping the State under the watchful eye of buzzing big oil biz, whenever not busy skirting bankruptcies. Still, elections can drive the economy here: one unlucky Sanchez 2002 Texas gubernatorial hopeful spent sixty five million dollars million to be top czar of The Lone Star. It happens big in Texas, and what a great way to recycle godly profits.

In a previous time, another Texan rose to the challenge of the White House. Racing to the line, Ross Perot spent Millions to flash his decks of cards, a hefty price for the sinking hole of the coveted name card. Whenever again fortunes abound, and pound the grounds for the highest ground, save your political buck and enjoy the sound of pounds making the rounds. Let it flow let it flow let it flow...

Looking Worldwide, Argentina may be on the mend with the IMF loosening the purse; Saudi Arabia is feeling left while oil is going right and Venezuela is going left. It remains to be seen where she goes next with much turmoil there, and we'll see who's right and who's left, shades of a new banana republic" looming on the horizon. Though Fidel still hasn't left, there aren't many places in the western hemisphere to be left.

Religion had a tough year in 2002: The Catholic Church is in pain with disdain, and Jerry Falwell is bidding farewell to his "Propheticities" on prophets, and professing to stay tame following unwarranted claims. Prophecy today can bring doom and gloom, let alone having to go in hiding and cocoon. Just ask one already masked ironman from Iran, the perennially hiding author Rushdie Salman.

Now that elections for Congress are past, and the GOP is in charge, we know who to blame, win or lose next time. Republicans are riding in style, conservatives head more to the right, while Democrats are scrambling to the middle to spread more rights. Centrist is the buzz word for everyone in 2004.

With elections not so far, and in contrast to his Dad, President Bush is riding his peak before a war, while Dad was at his peak right after the war. How to swing it, how to plan, drop out his deadbeat Treasury-man and fire up the bellies of the remaining Clan.

The Crystal Ball always waits to the last two weeks of the year because events are snowballing by then: Al Gore is punching out on Prime Time, fearing a new ripple effect of hanging nipples of ballot cards will deflect his winning punch-cards. And, still the one to fear, Hillary Clinton is lying low waiting for Desert Storm II to blow over, in hopes of landing the "Time's Woman of the Year", better yet the end of next year. And after 40 years in public Office, the past of the Senate majority Leader Trent Lott is surfacing to claim his future. Proof that the higher you get, the longer it takes your past to catch up with you, but whatever you do early in life calls the shots on you later in life.

One last note from The Crystal Ball on interest rates a year from now, if history can be a guide for this ever bewildering enterprise: once upon a time, a one term president famous for his 20% interest rates just got a Nobel Peace prize. It must be weighing heavy on the much younger president of our time, who can only muster a 5.5% rate. Foremost on Bush's mind is how to plan ahead and make a spike, to land this honor 20 years hence from now. The Crystal Ball will be on the lookout for spiraling rates to provide him the out from the present fix, and the inroad into the nobility crowd, and into the ultimate prize.

Imad F. Abdullah, December 2002

The Year 2001

2001 WAS THE YEAR OF the Big Bang.

One thing certain: whenever a big bang strikes multiple theories abound, gurus rule the waves and the stalwart expert upstarts fill the air with the wisdom of yesteryear extrapolated into the New Year.

And who can explain the bang when we're still arguing about the first Big Bang of multi-millennia of yore, when the first earth ball was formed.

No more hypes needed this year, it's all happening for real. Towers tumble down in a flash, a surreal event by any stretch. First gone One, then gone Two. Think of the years it takes to design and get such buildings up: the World Trade Center master architect Minoru Yamasaki was heard singing the blues, fortunate to have seen the grave before the WTC graveyard.

And in progress the Afghan Bang: whirling mullahs spinning in vain looking for a train out. Afghanistan is gusting bust and Kabul went kaput, and with pounds pounding pounds Afghan is in the bag. Hail to the chiefs proclaiming it "Happy Hour" time. Geography now gifted to all, compliments of war.

Democracy is going everywhere yet security nowhere. Flying the friendly skies, look out for them tailwinds as some planes dropped like flies. Hang on to your cell phone as you'll never know when last you may need it. But should it be and you get done-in, call from beyond and be the first of the living dead to break through dread and earn the distinction: grateful to be dead.

From Russia with love: in war as in peace keep counting your beads. Descending from the legendary Rasputin, the new Putin is the man: talking softly and carrying the Big Bear in his hip pocket. Russian Oil is on sale, OPEC get laid.

And there is another bang from a mighty one, symbolized as ENE also known as Enron... The higher they go the harder they fall... Houston, the oil capital of the world added a new first to its Hall of Fame: from 80 billion dollars to 26 cents in 80 weeks. Who says we can't make our own bangs...

2001 has also been the year of the wipos: equity gobbling monsters of 401Ks and KEOGHs and all the liquid green into their giant sucking machines. Retirement plans that already sucked were but captive audiences for them raiders of the sitting ducks.

And just in case you wonder who's the biggest of them all 2001 wipo-bangs? Her name is Darling CISCO, formidable wealth destroyer at 156 billion debit suck from starry eyed shareholders.

Back down to earth from the lofty heights of the

gone mighties and if you're in the market for office space, look no further than Downtown Houston. Class A quarters are at Enron bargain deals, energy included both in present value and in "Futures". Chevron-Texaco is unloading more feet, merger mania galore, and rates are for the asking for whoever is left standing to ask.

And if you're in for a sweet home after the stormy Allison Bang, look-out for the flood plain and check out the drains. Can't be too careful nowadays and FEMA insurance is the game. Mortgage refinance is in hot pursuit while the long rates are in swing and the Yield Curve is singing the blues. For shorts and longs of the lonesome bonds the thirty years are gone the way of Enron.

Nope, the Crystal Ball did not predict the Big Bang: it wasn't supposed to. But bang or not, The Ball was stellar in 2001: Last year's motto was "Sell low Buy lower, at least through March". And in sync the markets began to rise in April.

Though hit again on September 11, don't despair yet as the Crystal Ball will do the visioning thing again. In everything there is hidden beauty and the beauty about losses is the carry forward at $3,000 a year, forever... That is at least till your estate takes you over, a sobering thought for estate planners.

Back to the days of future yet to come, and back to the plus side. When stocks decline, there is a brighter side as they are cheaper to buy. When the art of the game goes up in flame how can you gain when it takes experts six months to call it a recession when it began 8 months ago?

Crystal words of wisdom: all stocks are worth buying but only after the dip, and we hasten to advice, on the deepest dip. How to get there if you're not already in? The name of the game is tenacity in the face of adversity and liquidity after the fall.. Buy in then sell out before the sell-out...

If you're still on the sidelines waiting for the signals again, time to stay offline at least through the Ides of March unless rocking high and low is your style and jiggling positions is your line.

Taxes in, money goes, Clinton comes, surplus grows. President Bush is in, tax refund and deficits grow.

Rich man can fly, the hobo stays in line, and food stamps come on-line. Keep an eye for one more mini-bang from Greenspan the moneyman before the return to the days of old when inflation ruled the world. Prices can only go up since they can't go down anymore and before they give away stuff with deflation. There may come the time when there really is a free lunch after all.

And who could argue when your bank rate take is two percent and your friendly credit cards tout the "exacticized" 19.87%? If you're in debt to your ears, rejoice for it is music to their ears. Get even, buy credit card stocks. And for the eager lot who bought cars with zero financing: zeroed in and zeroed out, beware the dealer participation sucking the difference.

By the end of 01, if you're wandering about the sinking middle class and where did it go, look no more. Some moved upscale dot.com style leaving the "didn't.come" to their fate. Silicon Alley turned to Death Valley and the Y2K revenge hit again. Some of the class leaped again to hobo land credit loaded and mortgage poor, thanks to cheap mortgage rates creating the phantom leverage. When time came for the leverage down, low rates were no help in lay-off lala-land. And when recession hits, equities fly faster than a blink and Class leaps are feats of fate, hostage to the Greenbacks of Greenspan after cutting the balls of the nasty inflation of the eighties.

Horizontal corporations are switching to vertical" again: the tough-skinned make bosses and the happy-go-lucky end up running out of luck. ENRON we'll miss you....

For 2002 The Crystal is eying The Houston Texans, perennials at heart, but new in start. Oilers in disguise they're not, but the rumors are about an infamous owner looking for a nametag on a stadium scouting for graces again. Enron Field may ring a new owner replacing Bud Adams Field.

Compaq is still here but the flight is near. Hewlett says no, Packard says why. Stockholders pray high: Fiorina, Fiorina, where art thou? CEO's come, CEO's go, Carly Fiorina which direction to go?

Houston has the same old for new mayor, re-elected by a 52% win margin, compliments of a promised future ride on the new railway to heaven. Hispanic Power was on the rise: President W had watched the high ratings of dad evaporate quickly before re-election time, and "Dubya" chose to support Hispaniola to build a wider base. Florida blues are still fresh in everyone's mind.

All aboard the Houston chou-chou train, and the artsy painted "Cows" are everywhere with gaucho artists riding them rodeo high. World-class Houston it is and Olympics are in sight, if and when the president thinks it's right.

As festivities get close and celebrations abound, relatives pour in to share the bounty. Fact is, that's how Einstein figured his Theory of Relativity: time and space are relative, and when you're with relatives time goes slower, and space gets smaller...

And no foresight will be complete without envisioning on the famous Houston Mosquito: turns out only females bite, and they prefer women over men, especially a pregnant one. Making babies has its downside and when you're outdoors stay on the run.

Until the next Crystal, Happy Holidays

Imad F. Abdullah, December 2001, Year of the Bang

The Year 2000

This is the Crystal Ball 010101

It's time to have a good dose of the hard stuff on New Year's Eve and kiss the infamous Y2K goodbye… Just as we barely made it through, imagine peaking now at the once and only one time in a Century, the "010101" also known as 010101.com January 1st, 2001.

And so it came and now almost gone, Y2K peaked on us a new century with all the doomsday hype and Armageddon, and the end of the old world biblical "predictantes" and predictors by now covering their butts with: "in the new beginning"…. Their "00" jinx was expected to destroy everything whatever and strangely enough, doomsday really fell on all those invested in the NASDAQ by last March, a cool pocket-breaking 45% loss since the Ides of March struck with a vengeance. Talk about the devil in disguise

Tech time switched to old economy tea time watching the early Sunset of the younger generation…. Throughout, the "Apples" and the "Dells" were chasing "Gateway" to seventh heaven, only to catch yellow fever slow sales and to stumble on Euro blues to seventh hell…. One hint to all who had plans of retirement for 01 and saw their 401K bumped back 10 years to four one one (411), get help and dial 411-GURU for the latest spin.

And what of all of them Dots? The ones with the ".com" behind? They fell like flies all Y2K after the great Cash Burn Rate was flaunted early in the year… Expect some at your office door begging after being paper tigers in the last century, with unemployment insurance first come first serve and foremost in their minds….(Dental included please…)

For most though Y2K was a good year except for Goodyear… Firestone is already on fire and Ford and Chrysler are burning rubber to stay afloat… The Germans are coming and Oldsmobile already punched out before another Chrysler style crash.

Yes "Y2K" was worse than predicted for some especially for all of you gas guzzling SUV machos pushing everyone off the road. On the plus side and as rumor would have it, better road manners come with the $35 per barrel price tag.

The "000" also played a numbers game in Florida. Too many enviro-greens and too many religions seem to confuse the adding machines on election day. By now you heard it all on the count and the genie is back in the box. You can rejoice if you have money still stashed after the latest markets run-down since President Bush promised a repeal of the estate tax. Great incentive to survive for at least the next 3 years it could take to become Law… It really pays to hang-in there.

By now you're probably wondering: how did the Crystal Ball do last year… Well it did, and just as the Crystal Ball always does, it predicted it where it counts and there is no contest yet. Last year's prediction was Buy High Sell Higher… It worked so well, at least through March 2000. This year, the new motto is "Sell Low Buy Lower"…. At least through them infamous ides.

This year there is no Biblical since there is a whole millennium to build up the momentum for the Y3K hype… In fact, Y3K could soon be upon us with time-compression.com racing us forward. They'll have much to claim that world collapse almost happened in Y2K, but that the 3rd time is the charm… No need to sweat it out as most of us will be bailing-out a bit sooner to watch from high above, hopefully.

As for other New Year predictions: all the gurus are at it and at least one will come the closest… (simple math here). Here is a sample advice for the leftover stock aficionados 010101, and one for the road: the NASTY-DAQ will be down from its peak but well above its low, provided Green-Fed Span Moneyman exercises caution and restraint in the face of up and "dot1.coming" new administration players.

Crystal clear, Texas will be riding high on President "W's" coattails and the scouts are already in contact with several 3rd world perennial icons for advice on how to better W's numbers in 2004, preferably how to get a sure over 90% and put the screws to them counting machines…

As for Houston, and as construction gets finished, we will have several domed stadiums to host a possible "in your backyard 2004 Democratic Convention". And with a President who made his fortunes in Oil and Sports Teams, it couldn't look any better for the oil / stadia capital of the world. Houston, the eagle has landed...again.

Until the next "Crystal", Happy Holidays.

Crystal Ball Greetings 010101, Imad F. Abdullah
December 2000

The Year 1999

CRYSTAL BALL GREETINGS AND IPOs' (Initial Public Offerings $$$$), End of 1900' $$$$

Just as we approach the end of time as all of us have known it so far, here is the real stuff beyond everything millennium that has already been published.

As reality would strike, little is known about "Y2.05K" or the still mysterious Y-1K. To correct this imbalance and with all the hype aside it's time for a serious look into the mystic and perhaps ride the carpet into magical wonder $$$$...

The Crystal Ball of the ages can go forward only so much, and back just so far. Looking ahead Y2.1 K (the year 2100) was too distant in the future for us non-performing below average non-centenarians... The Ball however was able to peak at Y2.05K (the year 2050), which I am hoping, some of us will get to see for ourselves (and nail that sucker in our twilight kicking and screaming...)

By 2050, and with no ozone to stop it, the then dinosaurus AOL so multiplied, split and zipped that it was able to penetrate through the celestial black holes and into the other side where the super-un-naturals reside. For the first time, us terrestrials are finally able to knock on the Pearly Gates for answers on where we're destined while we're still in the retirement planning stage"... Imagine the nest egg" needed to retire comfortably if we're granted eternal life"...

Further compounding the issue, new software from up-startling IPOs' (I Promise Only) is feeding the now monstrous and very mean Pentium 50, and is able to reach the beyond to Inferno.com and "Prophets-y'all.come", which as of late has become "Profits-y'all.income"...(Sinners with no money keep the hell out).

Speaking of gates, one more headline of 2050: Billy Gates Jr. (the 3rd), is bidding against Micki Jr. Dell, who are both by now "Zillibionnaires" after the latest stock run-up to buy the whole State of Delaware and its Corporate Registers for future IPOs' from "Sir-Dupont.sell", after the Enviro-un-Materialists final triumph over the evil chemical empire ozone busters of the last century.

Following on Stocks, the new motto for "Buy Low Sell High" has become "Buy high Sell Higher", simply because if you're not in the game you can't win but you're assured to lose. And here is a specific market tip before year's end: sell Coke and Pepsi stocks altogether as their pricing currently at .99 per bottle, will be .00 at Y2k and their value could collapse bezerkedly...

Now again, for the real important and timely of what to do come January 1, 2000: if you are stocking water and batteries, that's not where the real danger lies. According to the City Engineer in charge, it is the sewer plants that are not Y2K compatible yet and nobody knows when the fix will happen. Everyone is on his own if it starts backing up. Try the second floor and buy "PortaCan.Flush".

Back to The Future of Days Past: not much we know about what happened at Y1K, the year 1000, except for The Crusaders going back then to trace the holy footsteps in search of divine buried treasures. They probably missed the year 1,000 by 100 years or so, generations wasted in the trap of millennia one. Crusaders Y2K have an Intelli-Chip exacting Time and you can see the Holy Miss Molly from midnight Jerusalem live at 5 central time 12/31.

Again to the Crystal Ball of the ages, to year Y-1K (Y minus 1K), also known as 1000 BC or thereabouts: Much confusion about their who's who, when was what and where, and which Pharo did the Biblical. Historic maps show the known world as the Mediterranean and surrounds, most of Africa labeled Libya, a surreal reminder of mercurial ancestors of modern day galactics. Also in the map limelight Europe, Arabia and India, before map edges of early Greek cartographers plunge into oceanic oblivions. For us it was: America1492.Saved

For a look way back at the sacred "In The Beginning", the Crystal Ball is on standby for yet to come "GreatfullyDead-SeaScrolls.com" of early ages, and several "TimeMachines.coming" are racing the years backwards for a first look..... (keep your eye on the IPO ball). And to the first dawn 2000 gold seekers and if all else fails, there will be a final act lotto on Saturday December 31st, and what a start for a century if you win...

Present, past, and future, end of one grand century, and happy "Two Grand".

Imad F. Abdullah, December 1999

Epilogue

THERE IS SO MUCH happens each year that the Crystal Ball does not address although it may have been explored in previous years. Many events that are major and significant may only be facts that occurred and do not have the behind the scenes workings for the Crystal Ball to address.

The Crystal Ball does not try to predict the future but to forecast and envision where it might lead following an understanding of the events that already occurred. As we all of us receive basically the same information, the author does not recap the news but provides an insightful look on what may be significant that does not receive the necessary analysis and explanations as a result of the short attention span of the public, and the internal judgment within the media of what is important or captivating enough to have a wider exposure and dialogue.

Being The Crystal Ball makes one face-up to himself, his ideas and thoughts and his views on life and the world. One searches deep within for the meanings, and one is always in search of the input of other individuals with analytical and strategic minds. The Crystal Ball will come out again next December about the year 2012, and it will be reflective and visionary much as this book is and will continue the series.

The mind is our most precious permanent self, and my life quest is to continuously work at elevating my own knowledge and understanding in order to enjoy and understand the input of intelligent minds everywhere.

Imad F Abdullah, AIA